Heart of a Veteran

Ten American heroes sharing life stories of
service, courage, and resilience

Compiled by Jordan Holwell
Heart of a Veteran
www.heartofaveteran.com

DISCLAIMER

Heart of a Veteran is solely a compilation production of the individual authors, and the views and opinions expressed herein are solely those of the authors and contributors, and do not necessarily represent the views of the Publisher, the Producer, the Sponsors/Advertisers, or any of the other contributors of this project. Those entities make no claim as to the veracity nor the accuracy of any of these texts, nor do they provide any warranties or indemnities, either expressed or implied, due to the writings included herein and their implications on the Reader.

© 2016 by Heart of a Veteran
Publisher: DPWN Publishing
1879 N. Neltnor Blvd. #316, West Chicago, IL 60185
www.dpwnpublishing.com
Printed in the United States of America
ISBN 978 -1-939794-06-2

Table of Contents

Acknowledgements

In August of 2015, I sent my first email to a friend about the idea for this book. In my massage practice, I hear so many incredible stories of service, sacrifice and resilience from amazing men and women who serve our country and protect our freedom. I felt in my heart that these stories needed to be shared. My hope is that, by sharing the incredible journeys of these 10 veterans, others find the help and healing they need.

I would like to express my gratitude to the many people who saw me through this book; first and foremost to each of the authors for sharing their stories. Your stories have changed my life, and I hope will change the lives of all who read them. Thank you for taking this journey with me. I pray this process brought love, light and healing to your life. I could not be more proud of each and every one of you.

To all the corporate sponsors: without you, this grass-roots project would not be happening. Thank you for believing in me, Chicago Police Marine Corps League, Embody Movement Pilates, First Command Financial Services, First Community Financial Bank, The Greenberg Law Firm, McOriginals Creative Expressions and Photography, Pope Family Dental, The Price Group, Ray McGury and the Naperville Park District, and RHL Insulation and Fire Stop, and O'Callaghan's Pub.

To my amazing friends who saw the potential of this project from the very beginning: Julie, Ursula, Laura, Jen, CJ, and countless others; without you, this may not have happened. Thank you for keeping me away from the ledge.

I would like to thank Lisa Murtaugh Gangi of Elle Services for your mad editing skills and support of this entire journey, and Jody Bender for jumping in at the 11th hour to help. Kate Dever, of Kate Dever Designs, for your artistic vision and creating the perfect designs during every step of this project. You are a miracle and your journey with TBI over the past 3 years gives me strength and courage to get to the finish line of this project. Christie Ruffino of DPWN, for enabling me to publish this book.

My personal hero, Jason Billings USMC, you're always so supportive of all I do with the veteran community, and you always have my back. You were one of the first people I approached about this project, and you immediately jumped on board. Because of you, I've met some amazing men and women. Thank you to your wife and daughter, also.

To the ENTIRE team at the US Veterans Foundation! Jason, Greg, Chad ("Doc"), and Baron. Thank you for having the heart of a veteran and supporting this book, helping raise awareness for the 22+ per day. I pray the proceeds of this book will aid the US Veterans Foundation in helping veterans across the country.

Phil Noblin of Brothers In Arms Foundation... how can I even put into words my gratitude for your generosity and kindness? You are truly a hero to many for multiple reasons! Keep up the amazing work you do. I'm blessed to know you.

And finally, to my best friends, Lynore Taylor and Tom White, for your continued support of every single one of my insane ideas. Steve and Dawn Holwell, you are the best brother and sister I could ever ask for. And Lori, Niki, Sapphire, Josh and Mateo, it's great to come home to friends and unconditional love.

— JH

Resource Guide

Brothers In Arms Foundation

www.brothersinarmsfoundation.org

    Provides financial and logistical support to disabled veterans, active duty, and immediate family members of Marines & FMF Corpsman who have been critically wounded or fallen while serving within the Special Operations Community of The United States Marine Corps.

US Veterans Foundation, Alton IL

www.usvetsfoundation.org

ceo@usvetsfoundation.org

    Our goal is to help Veterans truly come home; our key objective is to address the epidemic rate of 22 Veterans per day who take their own lives and the disproportionate numbers of Veteran homelessness. There is a belief shared within the organization that every Veteran or Government Civilian Contractor who has honorably served deserves the future opportunities that they themselves have fought to defend.

National Veterans Search and Recovery

www.nationalvetsar.org

(202) VET-SAR0 (202-838-7270)

    Committed to locating and assisting lost or missing Military, Department of Defense Military Contractors, First Responders, and Law Enforcement victims and assist them into Recovery by offering resources, peer support and family support.

PROGRAMS AND ORGANIZATIONS

American Legion - www.legion.org

BraveHearts Therapeutic Riding Center
7319 Maxon Road
Harvard, IL
Phone: (815) 943-8226
Fax: (815) 943-8426
volunteerinfo@braveheartsriding.org

Homes for our Troops
www.hfotusa.org
(866) 787-6677 (866-7-TROOPS)
info@hfotusa.org

Iraq and Afghanistan Veterans of America
www.iava.org
National Headquarters
114 West 41st Street, 19th Floor
New York, NY 10036
Phone: (212) 982-9699
Fax: (917) 591-0387

Line of Advance
Chris Lyke
chris@lineofadvance.org
www.lineofadvance.org

The Mission Continues
1141 South 7th Street
St. Louis, MO 63104
Phone: (314) 588-8805
Fax: (314) 571-6227

National Veterans Transition Services, Inc (NVTSI)
4007 Camino Del Rio South, Ste 203
San Diego, CA 92108
Phone: (619) 822-2701
Fax: (866) 535-7624

Ride2Recovery
23679 Calabasas Rd. Suite 420
Calabasas, CA 91302
(818) 888-7091
info@ride2recovery.com

Silkies Hikes
BK Kang, National Silkies Hike Director
Irreverent Warriors
(770) 940-4165
www.IrreverentWarriors.com
www.SilkiesHike.com

Team Red, White, & Blue
www.teamrwb.org
1110 W. Platt St.
Tampa, FL 33606

Veterans of Foreign Wars (VFW) - www.vfw.org

HEALTH AND WELLNESS

Emotional Freedom Techniques (EFT)
Dr. Tim Carson, Pastor and EFT Practitioner
timothylcarson@yahoo.com
www.vetsallthewyahome.org

EFT is a healing modality to address any form of trauma, including PTSD or moral injury. The approach combines tapping on energy centers of the body, as used in acupuncture/pressure, exposure therapy and cognitive restructuring. EFT is performed together with a trained practitioner and taught for self help.

The Healing Place
Dr. Leona DiAmore
513 W 87th St, Naperville, IL 60565
(630) 946-6345
www.thehealingplace.me
2inspireu@gmail.com

Dr. Leona has been in practice 17 years. She uses a combination of gentle adjusting techniques and massage to clear out nerve disturbances that cause pain and dis-ease. If you do not like or are afraid of getting "cracked", release that fear, we can adjust you without cracking you. Dr. Leona offers very special rates for veterans seeking chiropractic treatment.

Higher Energy Massage Therapy
Jordan Holwell, LMT
www.higherenergy.net
jordan@higherenergy.net

Jordan Holwell is a licensed massage therapist, who believes in a holistic approach to healing. She is well known for her therapeutic massage work, and utilizes many different modalities and techniques. She also provides low cost massage and craniolsacral therapy for veterans and complimentary services for active duty military personnel.

LightWorks Energy (Naperville, IL)
Isabel Andrews, Reiki Master
www.lightworksenergy.com
(630) 881-8375
  LightWorks Energy, a Reiki and energy work practice, recognizes the fact that we live in an ever-changing world with outside and inside influences that affect our emotional, psychological, spiritual, and physical health.

Veteran Stress Project
www.stressproject.org
Nationally: Deb Tribbey
(707) 237-6951
deb@stressproject.org
  The Veterans Stress Project is an initiative of the National Institute for Integrative Healthcare (NIIH), a nonprofit research and teaching institution not affiliated with the government or any religious group. NIIH has conducted many scientific studies of EFT. Through our web site, we offer returning vets free or low-cost sessions using Energy Psychology, a method which many therapists and coaches are using to help veterans with PTSD to get their lives back. Go to the website to see television news stories about our work, and videos of veterans using EFT, the most popular Energy Psychology method.

BOOKS & MOVIES
- *The Evil Hours: A Biography of Post-Traumatic Stress Disorder,* David J. Morris
- *The Impossible Patriotism Project,* Linda Skeers
- *Project 22 Movie,* www.medicinalmissions.com/project-22
- *Soul Repair: Recovering from Moral Injury After War,* Rita Nakashima Brock/Gabriella Lettini/Camillo Bica (CON)/Herman Keizer, Jr. (CON)/ Pamela Lightsey (CON)
- *Tears of a Warrior,* Janet and Anthony Seahorn.
- *The Long Walk: a Story of War and the Life that Follows,* Brian Castner, Matterhorn
- *What It Is Like To Go To War,* Carl Merlantes

Foreword

It's estimated that 22 U.S. military veterans commit suicide every day, nearly one veteran every hour. We lose more military lives as a result of suicide than from combat.

This is not just a military issue; this is a community issue. Men and women of the armed forces make the selfless commitment to defend this nation's freedom, and then often return home feeling they no longer fit in. One veteran I worked with as part of my research on support services for student veterans relayed that once he returned home, he had no idea how he fit into the community that he once knew. Everything seemed different, and he no longer felt like he belonged.

The responsibility to adjust to life after the military should not rest on the individual veteran alone; this responsibility befalls us all. Fortunately, there is a multitude of ways to connect and support one another.

Through working with student veterans, as well as meeting with the veteran authors of this book, it is clear that each individual has a unique and exceptional story to tell. And yet, they all seem to share some common threads bound by their military service.

I frequently see a sense of fear and isolation, as well as loss of identity, as I speak with returning veterans, but I also see resilience, loyalty, and commitment to serve others. I see men and women supporting one another with the same sense of camaraderie instilled by their service, and contributing to their communities in a remarkable demonstration of resilience.

This past Veterans Day, I accompanied a college Veterans Club as they volunteered for an organization that raises and trains service dogs for veterans. When someone commented that they could have chosen to spend the day relaxing, as Veterans Day was, after all, meant to honor them, one veteran replied "As long as my legs still work, I'm going to keep working for someone else whose don't." It's moments like this that capture the spirit of resilience, the power of community, and the power of connection ingrained in these men and women. One veteran gained a sense of purpose and accomplishment while empowering another to gain a sense of independence, and hopefully, an understanding of how valued he or she is.

In addition to VA services, independent programs across the nation provide opportunities for veterans and civilians to lend support to transitioning servicemen and women.

Through intensive workshops, San Diego-based organization National Veterans Transition Services, Inc. offers assistance for veterans in making a successful transition into civilian life. Founded by military veterans and workforce development specialists, this organization provides aid for employment, career readiness and placement, and community-life functioning. The Mission Continues is an organization that empowers veterans by offering fellowships to support civic action and community service. Through this organization, veterans are successfully reintegrating by finding purposeful engagement and connection within their communities. Another organization, Team Red, White, and Blue, connects veterans to their communities through physical and social activity. The RWB Leadership Development Program allows veteran volunteers to enhance critical skills while organizing community programs that foster a sense of belonging within fitness activities and races. In Illinois, the US Veterans Foundation is a non-profit organization that helps transitioning veterans navigate through the constellation of services to ensure they receive the appropriate support during reintegration. And the Brothers In Arms Foundation is an organization that provides financial support to wounded Marine veterans and their families for expenses not covered by military insurance.

In continued support of the veteran community, the authors have elected to donate the proceeds of this book to the US Veterans Foundation and Brothers In Arms Foundation.

The authors of this book each share their own incredible journeys: stories of fear and courage, obstacles and triumphs, loss and redemption. Each story is as unique as the individual who experienced it, and yet, each story and each storyteller is connected – connected to one another and to you, the reader. Whether you are a veteran or civilian, you are bound to find yourself connected to another through the pages of this book.

And it is the hope of the authors that no matter where you are on your own journey, you will recognize that you are connected. You are a part of a community. No matter how isolated or alone you might feel, you are a part of something bigger. We are all a part of this community and as such it is our responsibility to support one another. This book also includes a list of resources and information about organizations that support veterans. We hope you will reach out for support if you need it, or reach out to support another if you are able. Regardless of who you are or where you are, we are connected by heart.

— Cari Stevenson

Professor of Psychology

Kankakee Community College

cstevenson@kcc.edu

Robert Canine

I grew up in a small town in Missouri. Like most small towns, there wasn't much for teenagers to do, but it was a good place to grow up. I was a pretty normal kid with a good upbringing. My parents were divorced, but that didn't seem to affect me. I have one brother and one sister; we are a close family. Growing up, I was an average kid. I wasn't particularly fast, big, or strong, and I wasn't that good at sports; I was just average at most things. I had a few things going for me, though. I did well in school when I applied myself; I had determination. I think I got that from my parents; they raised me well.

This is the story of what affected my decision to join and stay in the Army. In high school, I never thought I would join the military. Like most places, the recruiters used to come to the school and talk to kids about joining. At the time, I thought that was the dumbest thing. Who would want to do that? Luckily, a recruiter talked to me at 19, when I was a little more mature. I say "luckily," because it was probably the best move I ever made, professionally.

My life was mostly uneventful until around my junior year of high school, a time when I thought being cool and having friends was important. I made a few bad decisions, nothing major, from age 17 to 19. I started slacking in school because I found it boring, and my grades dropped. I would spend a lot of time with girls or hanging out with friends. Fortunately, I never got into any real trouble.

I graduated from high school and started working. That lasted about a year. I went to college for a semester and didn't like it. I seemed to lose interest in jobs or girlfriends after about three months. Nothing seemed to stick and I had no clue what I wanted to do. I was working a warehouse job when I met my Army Recruiter. He stopped me one day when I was walking my dog. "Um, no; no I don't want to join the Army," was my response. He continued and asked for an appointment so he could show me the benefits of serving. I agreed because I was getting nowhere fast at the time. I was 19 years old and ready to get out of our small town. I was unsure what I wanted to do, but felt I had to do better.

The recruiter came to my house and I was surprised to hear the pitch he delivered. It was great, and the Army looked awesome the way he told it. I was skeptical at first, waited a while, looked into joining more, weighed the benefits, and eventually decided to sign up. But it turns out he was right: the Army was awesome. It was probably a perfect fit for me. Several things drew me to serve, and I would recommend military service to most people; it's honorable and respectable, the benefits are great, the routine will keep you well-balanced, and the experience is immeasurable.

Everyone owes a debt to society; how you fulfill that debt is your choice. My choice was serving in the military. Being in the military is hard work, and the pay sucks, but I loved it.

I served as an Infantryman in the United States Army for 11 years, 3 months, and 12 days. I'm proud of that, and it would have been longer if I wasn't blown up. I lost both feet below the knee in an EFP attack in Baghdad. A reporter asked me, in an interview after I retired, "Was it worth it?" I didn't answer it at the time because I thought it was a stupid question, but I want to answer it now. You're damn right it was! If I had to do it over again, I would, but I would have taken a different route that night in Baghdad.

I joined the Army in 1999. The late 90s seemed pretty peaceful to me. This was before I had ever heard of any terrorist attacks or mass shootings. At the time, going to combat seemed highly unlikely. I chose Infantry as an occupational specialty for respect, excitement, and career advancement, in that order. The original plan was to serve four years, enjoy my time in the Army, and get out.

I went to basic training at Fort Benning, Georgia in August. When I got there, I thought I'd made a mistake by joining. The best way I can describe it was hot and painful. They have to break you down before they can build you back up. When I was at Reception, some idiot jumped off the top floor and landed on someone else. I guess he really thought he shouldn't be there. I decided to stick it out and make the most of it. I pushed the go button and kept my head down through basic training. Infantry training at Fort Benning was difficult but very rewarding when I graduated. One of my drill sergeants thought it would be a good idea to tell us what he thought of us right before graduation. He told me, "Some people lead, some people follow, and some people get out of the way. You're one of those guys that gets out of the way." That was true in basic training. It took me about one to two years to really be committed to being a soldier.

My first duty station was Fort Hood, Texas. The unit was First Battalion, Twenty-second Infantry Regiment, Fourth Infantry Division (mechanized), or

1-22 IN, 4th ID. I would later get deployed to Iraq with Bravo Company in 2003. We lost two soldiers in Iraq to direct combat action, SPC Powell and PFC Dervishi, gone but never forgotten, deeds not words.

I was a pretty average soldier for the first year or so of my career. After about a year and a half something changed, probably my leadership. I started doing well and began to enjoy the Army. This was around the time my son was born, and I started taking things a lot more seriously. I was driven with better purpose. I took soldiering seriously at that point and looked at it as a possible career. This is when I fell in love with the Army, the idea and its values, the idea of being a part of something bigger than you, the honor of carrying that flag. I love the Army because it taught me how to walk like a giant in the face of severe adversity; I learned this through outstanding leadership. When I first got to Fort Hood, it was peacetime. We were in the field a lot with the Bradley Fighting Vehicle and fielding new equipment they called FBCB2, basically an electronic map with your icon and other friendly icons to give you better situational awareness. We trained a lot from 2000 to 2002. 9/11 changed everything.

Everyone remembers where they were on 9/11. I was in the field. We had two squads of volunteers from our battalion in the field for three weeks for a pre-Ranger course. One of the instructors came over to us while we were planning a mission and we could tell something was wrong. He asked if anyone was from New York. Two guys said yes; he took them aside before addressing the rest of us. Those two went to call their families, who were fine. The instructor came back and told us that terrorists had slammed two planes into the Twin Towers. It was hard to believe that something like that could or would happen. Then he said, "Men, we're going to war." Although he was speculating at the time, he turned out to be right. It was different now! No more peacetime; this could mean we might actually go to the show.

I don't argue about why the U.S. launched the war on terror that put the military in Iraq and Afghanistan. Going into Afghanistan was a no-brainer; we had to go thump those guys. Iraq was questionable. To me, it didn't really matter, because I was a soldier. We were prepared to answer the bell; we weren't there to question why the bell was ringing. I think the attacks on 9/11 were an act of war against the U.S., and use of military force was required to eliminate the enemy. I think that any time a state-sponsored group attacks the U.S. to kill, injure, and maim innocent civilians, a significant military response is appropriate. You have to meet some of these people on the field of battle when faced with extreme terrorism, and that's exactly what we did. I do not value war, but I am a big supporter of the military and our veterans. They are an unfortunate necessity in defending our way of life.

4th ID was deployed to Iraq in April 2003. My son was two at the time, and I was a Sergeant, team leader, E5. It was difficult to tell him goodbye before we left, and even harder the second time when he was seven. 4th ID pushed into Iraq in April, about three weeks after the war began. We followed the lane cut by the Air Force and 3rd ID, and to be honest, the ground war was almost over when we got there. Our war, what I would call the war of insurgency, didn't start until around May 2003. The Iraqi Army was either destroyed or had fled, and we faced fighters determined to kill us, but not in conventional warfare. We became an Army of Occupation, and that is never good. We started getting attacked with roadside bombs and sniper fire. I understand the tactic – it would have been foolish for the enemy to meet us on the field of battle – but it was very frustrating. We were too well-trained and too well-equipped for them to match conventional tactics, so the insurgents fought an unconventional war.

After pushing past 3rd ID and continuing north, Task Force 1-22 IN was based in Tikrit, which was 1-22's "battlespace" in 2003. Bravo Company was assigned to a tank battalion, I think that battalion's name was 3-66 AR, but its battlespace was a little further north, in Baiji, Iraq. We were staying at a place called K2 airfield (if I remember correctly).

I am going to try and remember this story as accurately as possible, but sometimes I forget things. That could be from getting old, but getting blown up doesn't help. I've never been rated for traumatic brain injury (TBI), but here is the thing. They say those close-proximity blasts damage the white-matter tissue in the brain. We are just now learning about the danger of concussions; it's a similar process. When you are around enough of those close proximity blasts in Iraq or Afghanistan, sometimes you forget things. My last day in Iraq, I took a big one right on the chin… well, actually, on my legs, but the explosion was within 10 meters. I know that blast has affected me.

My platoon started running combat missions in Baiji and the surrounding area. This included raids, checkpoints, random searches, armored presence patrols, and the occasional contact with the enemy. There are a few events that stuck with me from my time there like a movie that can be replayed.

Roll film! We were on patrol one night, and had set up a hasty checkpoint on Route 1, just south of Baiji. You could hear sporadic gunfire in the distance.

Several civilian cars drove up to the checkpoint with bullet holes and said "Ali Baba," or thieves, had shot up their car and robbed them. After the first car, we thought it was a possible ambush. After the third car, we decided to investigate.

We traveled north up Route 1 towards Baiji with one Infantry Squad, one Tank, and two Bradleys (armored troop carriers). The tank in the front of the column reported contact with dismounted troops. The Bradley I was riding in stopped abruptly and dropped ramp. The Bradley commander told the gunner to engage; first with the 7.62 coaxial machine gun, then with the 25mm cannon when the enemy started to scatter. The firing ceased after many high-explosive rounds. The Bradley commander popped his head out of the hatch and said, "Go clear the objective." I hesitated and turned to my squad leader. He said, "Canine, take point." At the time I was scared, but didn't want to let anyone down, so I pushed the Go button and pushed forward. We moved out in a wedge formation after getting description, direction, and distance from the Bradley Commander, who was also the Platoon Leader. I acknowledged and moved out. I was terrified.

We walked the 500 meters while the Bradley covered us. It was pitch black that night and we were walking toward the city, so night vision wasn't much help. We could only see about 10 to 15 meters in front of us.

As we approached the objective, we got online to sweep across. The number two man in my fire team said, "I think I see something." I looked in the direction of his infrared laser and saw an object on the ground. It was hard to make out in the darkness, but as we approached I could tell it was one of the enemy combatants. He was right in front of us. I was so scared I didn't want to approach him. I said, "We got one right here." My platoon leader had dismounted his Bradley and followed the squad on foot. He shouted, "Search him!" I looked at my number two man and almost repeated the command, but I was so scared myself I couldn't tell him to do it. I told him to cover me and I approached the enemy combatant.

He was dead, but looked like he was faking. I nudged him with my foot; no response. Then with my rifle; no movement. Then a well-placed kick; still no response. I lowered my weapon and searched him as my soldiers covered me.

This event turned out to be pretty traumatic for me, and was one of the events that I think contributed to my PTS. I told myself that night that if I ever make it back home, that I'm never re-enlisting again. When I touched the guy to search him, I felt like it stained me; to this day I am haunted by this experience.

The guy I searched was killed by small arms fire. There was another enemy combatant that was killed with a 25mm high explosive round. The blast almost blew him in half. He still had a thin strip on the left side of his body keeping him together. The blast had blown off most of his clothes and made him defecate himself. Craziest thing I ever saw. I wasn't searching him! I already got mine over with on the first guy.

We cleared the objective and set up a perimeter. We called the Iraqi Police to come pick up the bodies. While we were waiting, the sun started to come up, and I moved to the middle of the perimeter. We left a soldier at the center to guard the enemy combatants. The soldier started make derogatory statements, in what I believe was a defense mechanism meant to desensitize the situation. The Iraqi Police picked up the bodies and we went back to base... End of mental replay.

We had a few other engagements in Iraq. I won't go into detail on the rest of these. That last one was hard to write about, because it was traumatic to me. These kinds of situations have affected our soldiers; I'm going to address that more when I talk about healing modules.

Yes, if you are suffering with PTS like I was, there are holistic healing modules that actually work! Stick with me here.

The first time we took contact, I was riding in the back of a Bradley. We were on night patrol on Market Street in Baiji. I was sitting in the back of the rear vehicle in a three-vehicle convoy. I heard several loud explosions and looked through the periscope to see a rocket propelled grenade, or RPG, hit the ground behind us and tumble over the Bradley. Several RPG rounds were fired, and the Bradley in front of us was hit by an RPG-7 right through the back of the ramp. All the dismounts in the back were spalled. My squad leader was yelling in the headset, "RPG ambush, RPG ambush!"

All three vehicles in the convoy were still drivable. We bent the corner to escape the ambush, the convoy stopped, and my Bradley dropped ramp. The Bradley Commander yelled over the loudspeaker, "Dismount right, dismount right!" I paused for a second and looked at my Squad Leader. It seemed like everything froze for some time, but I'm sure it was only a second or two. My Squad Leader reinforced the command to dismount right. I exited the Bradley with my fire team. We took some losses in this engagement, but nothing serious. One soldier was medically evacuated but I don't think his injuries were life-threatening.

I had a few other close calls on my first tour. I almost got run over by a bus attempting to run a checkpoint at 70 mph. I almost stepped on a land mine while on dismounted patrol. I saw a guy pass out from the adrenaline rush of being shot at. He might have just been scared, but I honestly think he passed out from the rush. Another night on patrol, the Bradley in front of mine was destroyed by a land mine. The blast was so strong, it blew the transmission out of the Bradley, and the engine access cover blew so high it knocked down the power line.

There were several other pretty memorable non-combat events from my first deployment, like when we had to burn the barrels from the makeshift porta-potty. (Don't forget to add diesel fuel and stir with the longest stick you can find.) Or, the three weeks we spent at what we called Camp Negligence: a dusty, open area where the battalion set up a defensive coil. It was the beginning of the war, so we didn't get resupplied for two or three weeks. I think the rations were down to one MRE (meal ready to eat) and two bottles of water daily. I can remember sitting in the back of a Bradley for hours on missions, just sweating from the heat. The conditions were tough at first, but improved over time, when our unit moved to the airfield. I got to come home early from that deployment. I separated my shoulder in a non-combat injury that required surgery, and was re-deployed back to Fort Hood. Shortly after the surgery, I came down with recruiting orders. I was selected by the department of the Army to be a recruiter. Sounds honorable, but I still think it is a crappy assignment, especially in 2006 and 2007 during the surge in Iraq. I did not like being a recruiter, but it is an important task for the military. It took me almost a year to get comfortable with the job. I tried to tell my recruits the truth about what to expect and give them accurate information to make an informed decision. I witnessed many young men and women bravely sign up despite the current events in Iraq and Afghanistan. Recruiting had a profound effect on my career. When I arrived for recruiting duty, I had made the decision to not re-enlist. I was going to finish this detail and move on. After witnessing such courageous acts, I found it too difficult not to re-enlist. I felt like I would have been turning my back on my recruits and fellow soldiers, so in 2007 I re-upped for 6 more years. We go to war for our country, but we fight for each other. The experience I had with my brothers in combat will always be cherished.

I was reassigned to Fort Riley, Kansas after recruiting. I was a Staff Sergeant at the time, an Infantry Squad Leader, the backbone of the Army... best job I ever had. My unit was Bravo Company, 1-18 Infantry, 1st Infantry Division. BCo was a strong and gritty infantry company at the time that went by the call sign The Barbaric. This was a mechanized unit, so I was familiar with the job. It didn't take me long to get back into the swing of things in an infantry line unit after recruiting. You have to fill some big shoes to be an infantry squad leader, but I was ready. The Army trained me, plus I had some outstanding soldiers.

My new unit was gearing up for a deployment to Iraq. I knew this when I chose the duty station. We spent a lot of time training in the field in preparation for the deployment. I got to know my unit and my guys better during this time.

We deployed to Iraq in 2008…battlespace, Baghdad; we were going to the show and hitting the big stage. Baghdad is a large city that often saw contact with the enemy. The Army was downsizing its combat force after the surge. Our company would be responsible for the area previously covered by three companies in northwest Baghdad. We stayed at a joint security station (JSS) called H2, which was a small warehouse district in the neighborhoods we were responsible for. If anything cracked off in our battlespace, then we had to respond.

The Army saw it as more beneficial to be embedded with the population instead of utilizing large bases. This was about winning hearts and minds. We were right there with the Iraqi people.

My company ran routine missions and presence patrols daily to enforce security. We were also responsible for the security of our outpost, so we rotated between guard duty, patrols, and down-time. Our area was mostly quiet, but you could tell it hadn't always been that way. The main road running through northwest Baghdad had multiple checkpoints to defeat IED or EFP emplacement. The opposition would attempt to attack U.S. convoys on a main supply route. Our map called it Route Vernon. We spent a lot of time patrolling this road and the three neighborhoods we were assigned to. Sometimes we traveled to the airport or Camp Justice but mainly stuck to our battlespace.

It seemed like you couldn't go 100 meters on Route Vernon without seeing a small crater on the side of the road from roadside bomb attacks. If friendly forces didn't keep eyes on these locations, then someone would try to emplace an IED or EFP. Things seemed to go off about once a month in Baghdad during our stay. I'm not exact on the statistics, but I'm sure the military still has that information.

I talked to the Sergeant Major of the counter-IED unit when I was recovering at Walter Reed. He said his convoy got hit on Vernon while we were there. Baghdad is a big city. We didn't have enough troops to be everywhere all the time. We tried our best and were at a lot of places. We definitely fought the good fight and prevented a lot of unnecessary violence. We are experiencing this now with ISIS, ISIL, or IS, whatever you call them. They, the enemy, are still around.

Before I got blown up, we responded to a different EFP attack on a convoy heading south on Vernon. My platoon was on patrol at a checkpoint about half a mile away. We could not see the road because large concrete "T-walls" were emplaced to prevent attacks, but we could tell a convoy was headed south, because the gun trucks had their spotlights on. My guys and I were paying attention to the checkpoint so we didn't get caught lacking, when we heard an enormous explosion. I turned toward the direction of the blast and could feel the ground shake. It looked like a convoy got hit but we weren't sure. There was no follow-on attack or gunfire. My platoon sergeant called it in, and we mounted up.

See, we didn't know, but we already knew. We were highly trained at home, in Kuwait, and in Iraq about these potential threats. We trained on how to recognize and defeat the threat, the procedures in dealing with these threats, and actions after contact. Plus, if you had been to the show before, then you already knew the name of the game: unconventional.

Information came back from higher headquarters on the radio that the unit had taken contact, so we moved to assist. The attack was on the south edge of our battlespace, close to an Iraqi checkpoint. Vernon was a four-lane highway for higher speed traffic, with T-walls on both sides, and had a side-access road. Most of the access points were blocked.

We approached their supply convoy and could tell the blast took down a T-wall. We still weren't sure if there were multiple EFPs, enemy combatants, or if this was a single-blast incident. We secured the surrounding area, assisting the convoy that was already in the process of casualty evacuation. We asked if we could help in any way, they said, "provide security, we have casevac (casualty evacuation) covered." The truck commander of the lead truck was hit with an EFP and he was down. I'm not sure what happened to him. I wish I would have asked his name for closure, but I didn't.

We searched the surrounding area on foot and went into a residence close to the blast, but found nothing. This event was a single EFP emplaced to attack the main supply route. Counter-IED units send specially trained soldiers to the site for site investigation, and they file the reports so the Army can prevent these attacks.

Northwest Baghdad was mostly quiet during our tour except for a few random events. My platoon patrolled regularly, usually every day. We rotated men and it broke down to a patrol three or four times a week. These patrols were normally four to six hours and consisted of providing a military presence in our area, engaging the public, assisting the Iraqi military, and talking to influential community leaders. Sometimes it felt like we patrolled simply for reputation. They call that "wasta" in Iraq, or street credibility. We had to be in our sector to enforce security during rebuilding efforts or bad things would happen. Our soldiers went fearless into the night knowing full well the dangers, and it was an honor for me to lead them for that brief moment. My biggest fear was letting them down, or letting my superiors down. I had some outstanding leadership throughout my career, and outstanding soldiers. I honestly feel like the EFP that got me would have been impossible to see from our vantage point, but I can't help but feel like I let them down on some days. Route security was my responsibility. I was supposed to be invincible like all the other squad leaders.

On May 17th, 2009, a U.S. combat patrol was attacked in Baghdad; the attack was initiated by an EFP. I was the truck commander of the lead vehicle in a four-vehicle convoy. We were in northwest Baghdad in up-armored HMMWVs (highly mobile multi-purpose wheeled vehicle), sometimes referred to as a Hummer.

When I think about that night, it always starts in the same place.

Cue film!

I was sitting in the front right seat. We pulled up to an Iraqi Army checkpoint at the interchange of Route Mets and Route Vernon. My platoon just finished a night patrol in our battlespace and we were heading back home to the Joint Security Station, or JSS, for the night. It was around 10 p.m. Baghdad time.

Roll film!

A blue car with two occupants sped away from the checkpoint as we pulled up. I looked at the Iraqi Army soldier standing in the road at the checkpoint. He quickly charged his AK-47 and we glanced at each other for a moment. His behavior was strange and I had a gut feeling that something wasn't right. I used to get these feelings often in Iraq. Like something was wrong or we needed to be vigilant. I had that feeling on this deployment at least 10 times before that night and it was nothing.

This time was different. I called my platoon sergeant on the radio and told him what I observed. We paused momentarily and then continued moving. I turned right onto Route Mets heading east. We were about a mile or two away from the outpost. There was nothing else out of the ordinary about this night or this patrol. Route Mets was a main road, four lanes, and had light poles at intervals. The four HMMWVs were traveling staggered column. My truck was leading in the far right lane. All the soldiers in the truck have a sector to scan for threats that is assigned by the truck commander. My sector was front right, close threats, including roadside bombs. We continued down Mets remaining vigilant for any threats.

That's when it happened. It came out of nowhere. Enemy insurgents had emplaced an EFP behind the concrete base of a light pole. They bury or spray paint them to disguise them. The only part visible is the clear window for a sensor that picked up vehicle engine heat. Fortunately for me, the "rhino" we had on the front of the vehicle set it off prematurely or it would have killed me. I never saw it and I was looking right at it. I heard the precursor charge, then everything went black.

The explosion knocked me out. I'm not sure how long I was out, but I came to when the medevac vehicle was talking to my driver through the window. Everything was slow and groggy, like a rebooting computer. I hadn't regained all my senses yet, but I could tell they were talking about who was hurt. My soldiers seemed to be okay, but I was a mess. Everything slowed from this point until I woke up at Walter Reed. I think my brain and body went into survival mode. It seemed to turn everything off except necessary life functions. It didn't hurt, I wasn't scared, or afraid I was going to die, everything just kind of stopped. I started thinking, "Okay, what just happened? Where was I before the lights went out? …Oh yeah, I was traveling on Mets, looking for an EFP, I heard a precursor charge…."

And then it hit me. My truck got hit with an EFP. I knew exactly what it was from that point. We had trained on these many times.

The EFP blast penetrated the 500-pound steel door on the HMMWV and hit me in the feet. I wasn't sure how bad it was, but I knew it was serious. I tried to open the door, but it was jammed against the curb. My weapon and radio were destroyed and I was pinned in the truck. I was leaking badly. One of my guys said it looked like someone dumped a five gallon bucket of paint on the ground.

My lower right leg was almost completely blown off, and I had a large laceration to the back of my left leg.

Two soldiers from the medevac truck picked up the door and swung it open. One of the soldiers said, "get out." I told him, "I can't, my legs are fucked, pull me out." They pulled me out and put me on the sidewalk. The medic was there and we started combat lifesaving steps. My right leg required a tourniquet below the knee and my left leg required a tourniquet above the knee. I was placed on a litter and we started taking gunfire. The gunner on my truck began to return fire in the direction of enemy muzzle flashes. The gunfire was brief; probably the enemy covering a hasty retreat, but I couldn't tell. I was strapped to a litter on the opposite side of the HMMWV.

Shortly after the gunfire ceased, I could hear attack helicopters overhead. I was loaded into the HMMWV that came up from the rear for casevac and we drove to the JSS. A helicopter picked me up from there and flew me to the combat support hospital in Balad. When I arrived they placed a mask on my face and I passed out.

And…Scene. End of replay.

They took my right leg off in Iraq – it had to go – and they took my left leg at Walter Reed; I was hoping I was going to keep that one. Live by the cannon, die by the cannon, and sometimes you get maimed. If it weren't for the quick actions of my platoon and company, soldiers and superior, and the awesome military doctors, then I wouldn't be here today. They saved my life with their quick actions; they were vanguards.

That was the end of my Army career, but the story doesn't end there. I want to talk about rehabilitation and about healing modules for veterans who may be struggling. This is why I wrote this story. I want to share it with other veterans with the hope that it may provide options for healing.

When I returned home, I wasn't the same person, and had trouble dealing with PTS, moral injury, and depression. I lost my feet and my career in a flash. I would have angry outbursts, impulsive behavior, and difficulty maintaining relationships. I was never suicidal; I just didn't care. I want to be careful not to add to the stigma of returning veterans so I'll keep it short: I was in the pits.

I battled with PTS and depression for 4 years after exiting military service, until I found hope. Everyone's path to healing will be different, but this was mine. You have to find someone you can trust. Share your stories with them, even if the stories are horrible. For me, it was my girlfriend. Education on PTS and moral injury was huge for me. My favorite book on PTS is The Evil Hours by David Morris, and the book on moral injury I like is called Soul Repair by Rita Brock. I found rehabilitation in the movie "Project 22," about veteran suicide.

Put purpose behind your Army story, and make it mean something. For me, I had to do it for my kids. I needed to paint this story as something positive that my kids can use for good. Military children serve too.

I think healing from PTS is a process that can be accelerated or decelerated, but there is a clear moment I can look back on and feel like I turned the corner. I had a big breakthrough with a therapy called Emotional Freedom Technique, or EFT, with my pastor at church. EFT was a very effective healing module for me. You can find more information on EFT at the website stressproject.org. There are several healing modules in the movie "Project 22" that I want to try, like meditation and equine therapy. I have heard from several sources that group meditation can provide healing.

I stopped drinking because I could never find the answer at the bottom of the bottle. To me, prescription medication is in the same category as alcohol. I know there is a time and place for pills, but killing your emotional attachments with drugs or alcohol only made things worse for me. When I stopped taking pills, I began to recover. I made small gains daily through exercise, good sleep, and eating well. All of these things I keep in a "rucksack" of items to offer to veterans for healing. I still have a lot of homework to do on this issue, and would like to add several more holistic therapies that have worked for other veterans. If you are struggling with PTS(D) or moral injury, please don't give up. There are healing modules that work. Continue to search for your spark and put meaning behind your story. It is ours to tell; we are the victors. ✧

Robert Canine enlisted in the U.S. Army in 1999. During his 11 years of service as an Infantryman, he was deployed to Iraq twice: in 2003 with 4th ID and in 2008 with 1st ID. On May 17th, 2009, a U.S. combat patrol was attacked in Baghdad, Iraq; the attack was initiated by an EFP that hit the vehicle Robert was riding in, resulting in the amputation of both legs below the knee. He was evacuated to Walter Reed National Military Medical Center, where he spent 18 months rehabilitating, and was medically retired from the Army as a Staff Sergeant.

Robert returned to Missouri after his military service and battled with PTS and depression for 4 years, until finding the spark that enabled him to put his issues with PTS behind him. After finding healing through holistic therapies and education on PTS and moral injury, Robert has been working to promote awareness and education on veteran suicide, moral injury, and PTS. Robert's military awards include the Combat Infantryman's Badge and the Purple Heart. ✦

Leona Di Amore

A Gift.

This is a story that was gifted to me by my best friend, Joey. The intention: to be thankful for those in your life. To help others the best you can. To learn from tragedies. To take what you have learned and make the world a better place.

By the time this story is through, you will see the divine role Joey plays in my life, and my role in his.

Memphis, Tennessee, 1984; I was 18 years old. Like most college students, I was just existing. I was attending Memphis State University, uncertain of my major. By day, I worked as a Medical Assistant. I enjoyed that, but my future on that path was limited. I spent evenings sitting in lectures, which was boring and seemed irrelevant.

I spent most of my time daydreaming about anything to break the monotony. I wanted my life to be meaningful, purposeful. I wanted to travel, meet new people.

One evening, while watching a TV commercial, it came to me: I heard something about Navy and adventure. In MY mind I heard: "The Navy needs an adventure," and I thought, "The Navy needs ME! I'm FUN, I want to travel, I've got nothing going on in life. I think this will be great! I should join the Navy." Sounds crazy, I know, but I'm impulsive sometimes, or maybe it was my "intuition" or a higher power whispering, "Go play," ...so off to the recruiter's office I went.

A few months later, my BFF Suzy was dropping me off as I was getting ready to "ship out" to Orlando, Florida for Boot Camp.

I wanted to do more than exist; I wanted to LIVE. I wanted some excitement in life when I joined the Navy in 1985. Little did I know what an amazing, serendipitous time that would be. Looking back, so much of who I am is a result of my Navy experiences. I had no way of knowing of the future impact that these strangers I would meet — strangers who became brothers and sisters to me — would have on my life. This is what shaped my life and guided me to where I am today: A Mother, a healer, a proud Veteran.

I completed boot camp in Orlando, Florida. I became very skilled at folding clothes, marching, and taking orders. Next came "A" School to become a Hospital Corpsman. Lucky me: I was stationed at Great Lakes Naval base, north of Chicago. This was a great time for me; I was meeting all kinds of new people from all over the U.S. On weekends, my new friends and I would take the train into Chicago, and enjoy what came to be known as "Leona trips."

You see, I grew up in the Chicago area, so I knew where all the cool places to hang were, so every weekend all of us sailors would explore new pubs and do all kinds of wild and crazy things. I met one outrageous Irish girl, Kim, and she was fun-loving like me. We became friends, had a lotta laughs, and so many good times. We helped each other get through school.

As is Navy life, after school, we went our separate ways. She went on to nursing school; I went back to Orlando to await orders. It's been MANY years since then, and yet Kim and I are still friends today.

Back in Orlando again, I was just waiting to find out where I was going to be stationed for the next few years of my life. Orlando was temporary, I knew. There is a saying in the Navy: "Hurry up and wait," and I was learning the meaning. There were hundreds of us in a "holding" pattern, awaiting orders. Station assignments are a crapshoot. The anticipation of where I'd be and who I'd meet made me antsy. I was awaiting a chance to travel to somewhere I had never been, to create a new life. I was gung-ho, just waiting to jump into "Navy Life."

It was during that time that I met this guy named Joey. He, like everyone there, was awaiting orders. Joey was a Navy Diver; a special kind of diver called EOD (Explosive Ordnance Disposal), generally considered Special Ops Navy Divers. They build and disarm bombs and do other covert activities. Hey now, that'll get a girl's attention! Needless to say, I was intrigued. He had a way about him. Calm and confident without being arrogant.

He was kind of a bad boy... you know, the guy who "dares" you to do things. And, this guy was funny as hell! Absolutely hilarious. We spent countless hours laughing over everything, and nothing. He had the gift of gab and storytelling. He was a true Irishman and proud of it. And did I mention that he was really good looking? He had a thin, athletic build, and dirty-blonde spiked hair, looking like Billy Idol with those green eyes...and his smile lit up his entire being. Nobody could help loving this guy.

He was special. You know when you meet someone and there is a natural connection? That was Joey and me. We were meant to be; I am certain that there are no coincidences. When I met Joey, I was a 20-year-old, attractive, single, self-professed rowdy Irish girl from Chicago who loved a good time. We were destined to be the best of friends. I knew that immediately.

By now, you probably are wondering if we dated. No. Not even a kiss. Our connection was much deeper than that. We were so much alike, I was the female version of him, we would joke. He was my brother from another mother, my Irish twin. When we were together, it was endless witty bantering back and forth. People would come and just come hang out to watch and laugh with us. Everyone around us appreciated the "show:" silly and playful, often inappropriate, with a wide range of content, but always FUN. We made the best of our time together. That's how we're wired.

It seemed like forever that we awaited orders. We made the best of those times; we brought our own good time as we waited.

We worked all day, and played hard at night. Many nights were spent dancing, drinking, and laughing often into early mornings. One weekend, Kim, whom I met in "A" school and ran wild with while stationed in Chicago, and by this time, was one of my best girlfriends, came to Orlando to visit. She was a riot to hang out with. That weekend, I introduced Kim and Joey to one another, and the three of us headed out for a wild and crazy weekend to south Florida. Oh my, we three, together; we made comedy. We had so much fun, laughed until we peed ourselves, and then laughed some more. We played like kids, not just this particular weekend, but many more. As luck would have it, Joey and Kim hit it off. In time, they became engaged. My best friends, happy together. I could not have been happier for them.

As for me, I didn't mind being single. Joey had a friend named Jimmy whom he was going to introduce me to. In the meantime, life went on and Joey's orders to his new duty station came. Joey was being stationed in Virginia Beach, Virginia with EOD MU2 and he was shipping out soon. I was bummed. My buddy was leaving me.

In the military, you learn that it's not about time together, it's about the connection. We are accustomed to moving around. Quality relationships with authentic people trumps distance and time. We shared the same values of patriotism, honor, loyalty, and freedom; love of our country, and choosing to serve her. These were the ties that kept us together despite the separation.

It was very sad, but I said goodbye to my friend. I didn't know when

I would see him again. I took comfort in knowing that Kim would keep us connected.

My orders arrived shortly thereafter, finally! There was to be no more moping around because my friend left me. I was moving on to my next chapter of my new and exciting life.

God has a sense of humor. I got my orders to my duty station to fill a role that had never had a woman in that position. Good thing for me I excel in a male-dominated setting; I'm not easily intimidated. I knew that this was going to be a real blast, as well as a challenge.

My orders were for a Navy Corpsman/Medic with a group called EOD (Explosive Ordnance Disposal) Group 2 in Virginia Beach. That's right – I was going to be stationed with Joey! I was going to be reunited with my Irish twin! Coincidence? No such thing. Divine order, as you will see.

We reunited in Virginia the summer of 1987, and it was as if we had not missed a beat. Joey, Kim, and I were back together, having our good times. It was during this time Joey arranged to introduce me to his friend Jimmy.

Now this is where things get interesting. Jimmy was stationed in Orlando when Joey and I were both there, yet we had never met. Joey then got stationed at VA Beach… then Jimmy got stationed there. I followed shortly thereafter. Strange, I know, but wait — there's more to this story.

Things were simple when I first got to VA Beach; life was good. I made lots of friends, had awesome bosses, Tony and Jeff, I loved my job and the people I was stationed with. EOD was a very tight community. After all, when you build bombs for a living every day, each day being alive is a great day! These guys taught me to celebrate life every day, as if it could be your last.

I became known as "Baby Doc." Despite being the first woman in that position, I earned the trust and respect of these guys. I was awarded multiple medals for saving lives while out on an operation.

I was "groomed" by then-Senior Chief Perez, a.k.a. Tony, and Lt. Jeff. These men gave me roots, taught me the old-school ways, and gave me wings to become the woman I grew into under their watchful eyes.

These were interesting times to be in the Navy, as it was the beginning of the Gulf War. During that time, Jimmy and Joey were each deployed. Two of my best friends were serving in a war zone. Praying for their safe return was all I could do.

When Jimmy returned home, he and I were married, and I left the Navy in the summer of 1992. The Navy relocated us to our next destination. Sadly, Joey was deployed and transferred all around the world. That's just Navy life. As a result, we lost contact for a time. Deployments, time away, war, separation… all challenges which ultimately lead to Joey and Kim's breakup.

War sucks. Not just the physical and emotional toll, but the scars it leaves on the soul. I experienced and lived with the "ghosts" of those who return home. Those who saw, experienced, and did the unthinkable. After all, it is war. They return home disconnected from themselves, unable to fit back in the life they used to have, in isolation, self-imposed orotherwise; maybe due to guilt, or sadness, or maybe they feel as if no one around them could understand. Self-medicating to numb the pain, to shut off the mind, is not uncommon. Depression or anxiety, to which the only answer in "Medicine" is medicine. The side effects leave them zombies, or violent, or suicidal. I became very familiar with the long-lasting effects of Post Traumatic Stress Disorder (PTSD). After Jimmy went away to war, the same person did not come back. Despite years of trying to reach him, save him, be a cheerleader, begging him to get help, I could not get through to him. Sadly, after 14+ years together, we divorced. I chose to help myself and my children.

As luck would have it, Joey and I reconnected about this same time. He was my lifeline. In my darkest days after divorce, we talked and talked. Me in emotional pain, grieving a divorce, starting to start over.

And I was Joey's lifeline as well. He had returned after multiple deployments overseas. He retired from the Navy. This was not by choice, but rather due to medical discharge. Joey had been in a parachute accident and broke his back in several different places. His "recovery" from this horrible accident consisted of the best medicine could offer: drugs. Drugs for pain, emotional stress, muscle spasms, and more. He hated it. He hated the medication and how it made him feel. He hated that that it was his only option.

It made me sick. This man who had dedicated his life, his entire career to protecting us and serving our country was left suffering and overmedicated. He deserved better than this. I knew I could help him. I knew I could relieve at least some of his physical, and definitely some of his emotional, pain.

"How did I know," you ask? It's what I do. When I was in the Navy, I became a Massage Therapist. After the Navy, I went on to teach massage. I was highly skilled; I worked on Olympic athletes in the 1996 Atlanta Games. I continued my education, and in December of 1998, I had become a Doctor of Chiropractic.

I served on an expert committee for The Department of Veterans Affairs for almost 5 years. I was appointed twice. During that time, I learned in depth about the VA healthcare system, and I consulted on policy and implementation of Doctors of Chiropractic in Veterans Healthcare.

I knew what Joey's VA options were, which were clearly not helping him.

I had been doing bodywork for years. As a Doctor of Chiropractic, I am an expert in Neurology. When I adjust, I remove nerve disturbances with specific adjustments. I know when nerves are stressed and compromise function. I know what parts of the nervous system cause chronic headaches, depression, sleeping issues, and pain. I do this all day, every day, in my private practice. I could help him! I was going to fix my friend.

We talked about his struggles, and we planned for me to visit him in June of 2010. This would be an awesome bonus trip as well. Despite years and distance, I convinced Joey to reconnect with Kim. He did, and they had a once-in-a-lifetime experience. I was so looking forward to his recovery, and to helping my brother! To seeing him heal. To seeing him happy and to seeing that smile. I knew I could help him. I even did research at Camp Pendleton on the worst of the worst cases of PTSD, and found amazing results. Helping him to heal became my secret obsession. After all, he was like my twin... I had to make this right.

I never did get that chance to help him. Joey committed suicide in May of 2010. One month before I was planning to see him.

He was a war hero, a career military man. What a tragedy; I felt helpless, and guilty – why hadn't I done more? I could only shame myself that I should have made time to make him a priority.

The HUGE hole in my heart filled with a sadness I had never before experienced. Learning of his death devastated me. His passing was more devastating to me than the loss of my parents. The loss of Joey was compounded by the fact Kim was the one who told me of this tragedy. My heart broke for her as well; I knew she still cared about him and had reconnected with him. Both she and I were filled with so many emotions. This man deserved to live a full and vibrant life after having served this country. How could this happen?

Part of my heart died with him. As I write this story today, tears stream down my face. What a senseless tragedy. My greatest regret in life is not having made time to spend with him sooner.

How do you move on from something so tragic? Give thanks.

I thank God that he came into my life, and I thank Him for the love and laughter through the years. Joey was a gift in my life. Our friendship transcends time and space. In the quiet moments, I hear him, I feel him. His spirit is so bright and bold, and he lives on.

This tragedy has shaped my life today. I could not save my friend. However, I can save others. I can take this experience and help others, and I do. I serve Veterans with PTSD in my practice at no charge to them. I am an outspoken advocate for Veterans. These patriots deserve the kindness and care that they so desperately, and often silently, crave. It is my life's mission to continue to be the voice to advocate for holistic options in Veterans' health.

When we look back on our lives, we see the order in what seemed at the time to be chaos. The blessings of meeting people who start as strangers, then come to have such a profound impact on your life and who you become. The Navy was full of blessings. My Senior Chief Perez from VA Beach, Tony, is the Godfather of my daughter, Alexis. He is also a legend of sorts: he worked his way up from enlisted to a Commander now – making history with 43 years and still serving in the U.S. Navy. As for Lt. Jeff, he gave me an opportunity to help those with PTSD: he is both a Pharmacist and Psychiatrist, and he cares so much about the soldiers he brought me, the Holistic Doctor, to help them. Both of these men are still my best friends, even 27 years later.

There are other "shipmates" whom I met on my path, like Mike Monty, a Navy pilot who became my son's godfather. There there is Kim, with whom I still talk today. She serves Vets as a Nurse working for a VA Hospital. Life takes us to curious places. If you are as blessed as I am, you will look back and see that life is a gift. The characters, the stories, the memories, the laughter, and the teams are the whipped cream with chocolate and nuts on top. Savor it all! It makes you YOU!

All the good and bad experiences – ALL of them – have made me who I am today. I am fully aware that Joey was a gift in my life. This tragedy made me aware of being kind, compassionate, and passionate about reaching out to Vets. Telling them what I know as a doctor, loving them like a mother, yet respecting them as one of my own. I have learned that people may be suffering behind that smile. I was unable to help Joey; but NOW I'm helping others as a result of this experience. I will never turn away any solider with PTSD. In a strange way, taking care of them helps me to heal, too.

I choose to honor my friend by advocating, educating, being a light, giving hope, using my skills and talents to help the heroes among us. I'm just getting started. My role will evolve, be it VA reform, and maybe even a political route.

Our soldiers deserve to be cared for, have resources, to be treated with respect and dignity. These men and woman served OUR country. Look around you, and reach out to Veterans; they most likely will not ask for help. We live and learn. Your kindness and effort could save someone's life.

In my quiet times, I feel his presence; I hear him saying, "Girl, you're crazy," and I can hear him laugh. I know he's passed. I also know energy NEVER dies. It changes form. Similar to the "death" of a caterpillar, until it becomes a butterfly, I feel Joey in spirit; he is healthy and at peace. I know he's guiding me. When I think of him, I am inspired to help heal, and to make the world a better place. This is my gift to, and from, Joey. ✧

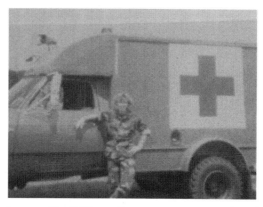

Leona Di Amore, Hm3 Navy Corpsman, was stationed with East Coast Explosive Ordnance Disposal 1987-1992. She served as the Medic to this elite group of Naval divers/bomb experts. She also traveled on operations and training exercises, then was awarded a Navy Achievement Medal for Life-Saving Measures as a result of a situation on an operation. After serving in the Navy, Leona returned to college and became a Doctor of Chiropactic in 1998. Since that time, Dr. Leona has worked with and volunteered with Post Traumatic Stress Unit at Camp Pendleton, California. The focus was to eradicate neurological stress which is associated with PTSD. ✦

www.thehealingplace.me

2inspireu@gmail.com

Christo Dragatsis

I was born in Joliet, Illinois, on July 31, 1930 to Greek immigrant parents born in Turkey.

I entered Joliet Township High School in 1944, at the height of WW2. I was fascinated with the Army, and joined ROTC and became a part of the rifle team. By the time I graduated, I qualified as a Marksman. I continued my education by enrolling in Joliet Junior College, graduating with an Associate's Degree in Business Administration in 1950. I was to enroll at the University of Illinois for my junior and senior year, and earn my Bachelor's degree in Business Administration.

The old National Guard was activated into the U.S. Army in 1940, to serve for the duration of WW2. I was recruited in 1947 to join the new local unit, Company G, A Rifle Company, 129th Infantry Regiment. I told them I would join on one condition: to train as a Sniper because of my Marksman qualifications. I enlisted at 17 years old on that basis. We met every week in 1948, '49, '50 and '51, plus two weeks of summer training on an Army base. In 1950, the Korean War started, and our unit was primed for call up. This is why I never finished my education.

Upon our return from Camp Ripley in Minnesota , our company, along with another, was called up by the Governor for riot duty in Cicero, Illinois, as the local, county, and state police were overwhelmed by what later came to be known as The Cicero Race Riots Of 1951. We were on active duty for 3 weeks and settled the riots.

In September of 1951, we were notified that the entire 44th Division would be called up for regular duty. I had already started my studies to become an officer in the National Guard. In November of 1951, I was activated for National Guard Officer Candidate School, and left for Camp McCoy, Wisconsin, to complete my studies.

I was commissioned a 2nd Lieutenant on January 27, 1952 and into the regular Army two weeks later, on February 15. My assignment was with Company E as a Platoon Leader at Camp Cook in California (Vandenberg Air Force Base). In March, I attended a 3-week course on explosives at Fort Ord, California. In April, I attended an Officers' class at 6th Army Headquarters for three weeks (which was CBR: Chemical, Biological, Radiological School). Halfway through, the entire class flew to the desert camp called Frenchman Flats, Nevada, for further training, and witnessed a live atomic bomb explosion. Then we returned to class back in 6th Army HQ in California.

Upon finishing the course, I returned to Camp Cook for further assignment. For 5 months of early 1952, I and 5 other Infantry Officers attended the Armored school in Fort Knox, Kentucky, and by the time we returned to Camp Cook, my original unit had been shipped to Korea.

While in active duty, we were charged $1.75/day for meals, which was deducted from our pay, and we initially had to buy our own uniforms, for which we were reimbursed 6 months later at half-cost for an Officer's Uniform.

In November 1952, Camp Cook was closed and the remaining men were shipped to Fort Lewis, Washington. On December 20th, I was assigned to Korea as an Infantry Officer to Company E, 23rd Infantry (Manchou) Regiment, 2nd Division.

On December 25th, I joined my unit on the DMZ (Divided Military Zone) as Platoon Leader. It was 20 degrees below zero for the next 10 days and we were camped in 2-men foxholes. There was no fighting going on, but there was gunfire. I didn't wear my gloves all the time… and I got frostbite.

We called this home: Hill 233. For the next 7 months, we conducted combat operations on the front line. During those 3 major battles — Bloody Ridge, Wosan Corridor, and Jane Russell Hill (because it looked like two large breasts) — it was combat operations every day for 7 months.

The Chinese attacked our position every day, but we would not budge. The slaughter was unbelievable; the Chinese suffered over 1 million casualties. I kept on praying that I would reach my 23rd birthday on July 31st, 1953, without being wounded… or killed. The armistice was signed on July 27th, 1953 — 4 days before my birthday. I survived 7 months of combat without a scratch. Living conditions improved: hot meals, tent living, a shower every 2 weeks. We were on alert all the time.

In August 1953, I was promoted to 1st Lieutenant to Tank Company, 23rd Infantry as an executive officer. We had brand-new M47 Tanks; life was bearable. In October of that year, I was promoted to company commander and remained there until I returned to the United States in August, 1954. I had served in Korea for 18 months.

Back in Fort Lewis, peacetime Army was a piece of cake, until I was discharged and transferred to the reserves for 7 additional years.

My last six months at Fort Lewis were fraught with accidents. I shipped my company of 22 tanks by rail to the Yakima training center for six weeks of winter training. In training one night, we were firing our 90mm cannons, with night vision, at daybreak. I opened up my hatch for fresh air and gave my crew a break. I stepped out of the turret and on to the deck, and commenced firing. The 90-mil shell was defective and we had a breach block explosion; I was blown off the tank with facial injuries. I was in the hospital for 6 days and had braces on my teeth for six weeks. Unfortunately, my gunner and loader were killed.

Two weeks later, as two platoons of my tanks were being escorted to the firing range by a young range officer, I told him that an escort was not necessary because we knew where to go. The roads were rutted and very dusty; visibility was zero. His jeep got stuck, and the first 4 tanks rolled over him before we knew what happened. He and his driver were killed. A big investigation went on for months, because he was following orders.

During that period, we had many accidents with our tanks, and after 6 weeks we shipped our unit back to Fort Lewis. I finally was discharged to go back home on January 31, 1955. 38 months of service during the Korean War and 18 months in Korea. I had not seen my family in over 3 years. My mother, aged 53 and all of 5 feet and 125 pounds, met me at the door. Her hair was completely gray. I picked her up and said, "What happened to you?" She said, "When you left for the service, I decided I would not color my hair until you came home safe and sound."

I had plans to return to college and finish my last two years, in order to get my degree in Business Administration at the University of Illinois. I was 24½ years old. Guess What? I thought I was too old to go back to school, with all expenses paid, through the GI Bill.

When I was discharged and sent home, I was making $235/month as a First Lieutenant. Two weeks later, I was hired as an Administrator at Blockson Chemical Company at $500 month. WOW! A year after that, I was promoted to Assistant to the Senior Vice President of the company, the job I held until he passed away.

In February 1956, my mother passed away. In the summer of 1957, I met the woman who would become my wife, Mary, at a wedding. We dated, and on Christmas 1957, we got engaged. On June 28, 1958, we got married (this year, we celebrate our 58th wedding anniversary). In 1961, our daughter Ann was born; in August 1962, our daughter Stacey was born; in March 1965, our son Mathew was born; and in February 1968, our son James was born.

Upon the passing of my boss, Ed Block, I was offered a job at our corporate headquarters in New York City. We flew to New York City to assess the situation; office, commuting time, and housing; we decided not to take the transfer, but rather, stay in Joliet, where we had family.

In 1962, I made a career change. I entered the insurance business, in which I worked for the next 42 years. During that period, my partner and I had a very successful business, which gave me the time to do other projects.

I was always interested in construction, and thusly became a real estate developer, building apartment and office buildings, and a shopping center (Shorewood Plaza). At the same time, I got involved in several City of Joliet projects, six of which have been most successful. First was saving the Rialto Theater, of which I was Chairman of the Authority for 14 years. I was President of the Joliet Junior College Alumni Association, which I served for 13 years. I was also involved in saving the Union Depot in Downtown Joliet, keeping Joliet Township High School open, and after a disastrous fire in the East side library, it was decided to rebuild the library, repairing the fire damage and doubling the building's size. The decision was based on the fact that there was a brand new library on the West side. There was also a special project in my neighborhood: Joliet Catholic High School was closed and the student body was consolidated with St. Francis Academy and moved to a new facility on Larkin Avenue. With neighborhood assistance, the old high school facility was converted to a senior citizens complex. All six projects are alive, well, and prospering.

In 2015, I was fortunate to be nominated for, and awarded, the Pride of Joliet Award, in recognition of all the work I did on various projects within the City of Joliet. ✧

Christo Dragatsis entered the U.S. Army in 1947. He started in the 23rd Infantry Regiment, became an officer in 1951, and served in Korea from December 1952, until August 1954, transferring from Infantry to Armored in 1953. He was 1st Lieutenant from 1953 until his discharge in 1955, and was Company Commander of Tank Company, 23rd Regiment, from October, 1953, to January, 1955. ✦

Phone (815) 355-1353

Jack Erwin

Bayonet Five-Five

    I enlisted in 1989 after my freshman year in college. I wanted to use the G.I. Bill to pay for my schooling, so that my younger sister would be able to go to college the following year. My family just couldn't afford both. I also wanted to serve my country, and I enjoyed challenging myself and proving to myself I had what it takes to make it. After all, playing football in high school and for a year in college was challenging yet fun, and it felt great to be a part of a team. I loved being outdoors, shooting, and going on adventures. I suppose it's best to fight a war when you are a young man, think you are invincible, and don't yet have a family of your own. It just didn't happen for me that way. After I returned from Army boot camp at Ft. Jackson, SC, the US invaded Panama. It was over quick, and done with overwhelming force, thanks to the likes of General Colin Powell. But I went back to school and started serving one weekend a month. Eventually, I joined the R.O.T.C. detachment at Ohio University and pushed myself to learn as much as possible to work my way up through the ranks. I wanted to become an Army officer and to be a good leader for my men.

    About a year later, our first war with Iraq came with the Iraqi invasion of Kuwait. While "Desert Shield" kicked off in 1990, I was at Ft. Benning with my buddies going through Airborne school to earn my beret and jump wings. I distinctly remember standing in formation about half way through the course when the soldier standing next to me, and quite a few others, were immediately pulled out of the course and told to, "Pack your shit! You are going back to your unit TOMORROW. Your unit is on alert, and deploying for combat." The pucker factor increased exponentially. That night, some of the "Black Hats" or Airborne instructors pulled the fire alarm at about 0200hrs and we were due to wake up 0430hrs to head to the terminal to draw our chutes and make our first jump. As it turns out, I was on the top, and my bunk was located right next to the fire alarm. I was having a bad dream; out in the desert in the middle of the night, unarmed, and fighting an Iraqi soldier with a knife. I was asleep when the alarm went off, the shock of it knocked me out of bed. I woke up when I hit the floor, but landed on my tailbone! Fight or flight kicked in and I immediately jumped up and started punching, kicking, and screaming. The whole platoon rushed down the hallway and into my room to see what the hell was going on. One of the Marines flipped on the lights, and I froze with my fists clenched saying, "What the f&$% is going on!?" It's just a fire drill, dumbass. "Oh, OK." Luckily, I didn't hit any of my roommates in the dark and we evacuated the building before any of the NCO's came in. Actually, it was good training, later in Afghanistan, I would be wakened in the middle of the night by enemy fire, and had to roll out of bed ready to fight. A few hours later, we ran to the terminal, drew our parachutes, and made our first jumps. On the next jump, we left the bird a little too late. So, my training kicked in and I "slipped" one of the corner risers on my chute so I could "fly" towards the LZ (landing zone). I did the longest chin up in my life and I made it. But the guys behind me landed in the trees. On a different jump, I didn't leap out far enough, and my risers spun around in a big knot, even though my chute opened. My training kicked in. I immediately started doing a "bicycle kick" and started my risers to spin around in the other direction. It worked like a charm and it was smooth sailin' the rest of the way down. I have to admit, I loved the adrenaline rush of jumping, plus the peace and tranquility during the descent. Risking your life somehow makes you feel a little closer to the man upstairs, and reminds you of your own mortality. Afterwards, someone told me my hand was shaking but I wasn't even aware of it. So I did my best Napoleon, and stuck my hand in my pocket until it stopped. Suck it up, Soldier! Move out!

I went back to being a weekend warrior and went home to college that fall. I went down to Gamersfelter Hall one day to do my laundry. It's a coed dorm, and that's when I met the love of my life. They have study tables set up so you can do your homework while you wash your clothes. Naturally, being a "Five Jump Chump" fresh out of Airborne school and full of swagger, I was not my normal shy self. So I sat down at the table across from three cute college freshman girls. I had to read some stupid book for my American Lit class that I had already read in high school. It was *The Scarlet Letter*. Anyhow, I was eavesdropping on their conversation, not reading, of course. I must have had a grin on my face, because Leila chimed out, "You're not really reading that book, are you?" That threw me a little, so I said, "Oh, well yes of course I am." (Way to go, Cassanova!) She responded, "So, why are you holding it upside down then?" (Doaoooohh!... She caught me.) We all started laughing and hit it off from there. She blinked at me with those long beautiful eyelashes and her pearly white smile that I just couldn't resist. She had a sarcastic sense of humor. So we chatted for a while and I folded my laundry and went home to do my other homework without thinking twice about it, after all, I already had a girlfriend. Little did I know, Leila would later be my wife and the mother of my two children. A week or so later, I went out on a Thursday night with my buddies. As soon as I walked across the dance floor to go to the john, I heard a girl call my name, "Jack!" As soon as I turned around, there she was; Leila, with her long eyelashes, kiss-me lips and a smile a yard long. That was it for me! I dropped my buddies like a brick and learned to dance as best I could. I insisted on being a gentleman and walked her home so she would be safe. There we were, standing by the freshman girls' dorm, and I suddenly only know three vocabulary words. And she kissed me! She gave me her phone number, but I didn't have a pen. I start repeating it over and over in my head until I get home. As soon as I walked in the door, I grabbed a pen and wrote it down. I didn't call her for about a week. I shouldn't have been calling her anyway, remember, I already had a girlfriend. One night I put on a pot of coffee so I could pull an all-nighter and type up a paper. At around midnight my girlfriend comes over while I'm typing and breaks up with me. Oh well, I had bigger things to worry about anyway, we are sending more and more troops to Saudi Arabia every day and my unit could be called up anytime. Even though I was brave enough to go fight a war, I was barely brave enough to call Leila, but I did. Once we broke the ice, that was it, I was head over heels in love.

We exchanged addresses and said our goodbyes as we went home over break for the holidays. She wrote the most touching, beautiful letters to me about how worried she was that I was going to be called up. Wow! She actually cares about ME! So, I grabbed my sister and took her shopping with me, because I needed her expertise on buying Leila a Christmas gift. We finally returned to campus in January. She bought me a gift, and I, in turn, gave her hers. But the biggest gift of all, was that we were in love. I decided right then and there that I wanted to marry her. If my unit was called up the next day and I was sent to war, I wanted to be married and make sure she was taken care of properly. Things started to get more intense as "Desert Shield" ramped up to gradually become "Desert Storm."

So in mid-January of 1991, President Bush came on television and let loose the dogs of war. Desert Storm kicked off and 100 hours later, it was over. Again, thanks to Vietnam veterans like General "Stormin' Norman" Schwarzkopff we used overwhelming force to decisively achieve our objectives, and then get the hell out...notice a theme here? Strategically, Iraq was a good balancing power against Iran, thus keeping the Middle East contained for a while. Kuwait was liberated, UN authority utilized properly, and the Iraqi army got a good ass whoopin' from the combined arms conventional might of the US military, as it should be. But, unfortunately, our enemies learned not to fight us that way, that they should instead use terrorism, guerilla warfare, and propaganda. After all, it worked great in Vietnam, and there was this new thing called the internet, which made it so much easier.

Leila and I enjoyed our time together. I went home to meet her family over spring break. One day, I dropped down to one knee in the park and asked her to marry me. She promptly said no, and I reached down and picked my heart up off of the ground. She was only nineteen. I saw things in black and white. She saw them in shades of gray. I decided to wait until she was ready. I graduated with my Bachelor's degree in Education in the fall of 1992, and finally earned my commission as a 2LT. It was a proud day. My Dad pinned me on one side, and my uncle Ted, a Vietnam Veteran, pinned the other, AND gave me HIS old jump wings to wear. I was now a "Mustang," an enlisted soldier who worked his way up through the ranks to become an officer. Shortly thereafter, I shipped out to Ft. Sill, OK, and spent the next five months learning to be a "Redleg!" That's where the best Field Artillerymen in the world are trained. I made "Commandant's List" for graduation and returned home to my Army National Guard unit and looked for a civilian job while I waited for Leila to finish college.

Her senior year, Leila flipped things around on me and asked me to marry her. I said, "This must be your way of saying, 'Yes'." We called our parents and were engaged. We married at Galbraith Chapel on campus July 15, 1995. We would be together for 23 years, 18 of those married. I always thought it would be for keeps.

I scratched by as a substitute teacher for two years and coached football at Nelsonville-York HS, hoping to find a full-time teaching position at some point. Meanwhile, President Clinton fought an air war in the former Yugoslavia, and dealt with drug lords in Somalia, and then an annoying little terrorist group called Al Qaeda. The two embassy bombings in Africa, Khobar towers, and USS Cole should ring a few bells in your memory, plus the "first" attack on the Trade Center in New York, when they set off a car bomb in the basement. Most people didn't pay attention, too busy with American life, and counting on a volunteer Army to stand watch over them.

Leila and I also enjoyed the lush American life. She found a job doing legal aid in southern Ohio, and I found my first full-time teaching job in South

Webster, Ohio. We worked in Ohio for about four years, and then she took a job with her aunt at a small law firm in Naperville, IL, so we moved to the Chicago area, and I transferred to the Illinois Guard. We drove a Ryder truck to Illinois and within a week I landed a job at Wheaton North HS and started coaching football again. Then, BAM! She was pregnant with our first child. She told me when I came home from my first day of school and I beamed with pride. Annie was born on May 2, 2001. She's my beautiful little redhead.

You know what happened next, September 11, 2001, and that changed everything. I distinctly remember sitting at my desk in school, grading papers. Another teacher came in and turned on the TV. "Hey, Jack, did you hear what happened? A jet crashed into the World Trade Center!" As we both stood there wondering how it was possible to "accidentally" crash a 737 into a skyscraper, we saw the second plane hit. I knew right then that it was no accident. "This is a well planned and executed attack, not an accident." I called my unit. We didn't know what to do other than pack our gear and be ready for the call. The next morning, I stood by the flagpole in front of our school at 7:00 AM while high school kids held a candle light vigil, prayed, and cried because they were scared. I had always wondered about the motto on the US Army's flag, "This We'll Defend!" At that moment, I finally got it. Damn right. This I will defend. My first alert came when Annie was 7 months old. By then we already had soldiers from our unit pulling armed security at O'Hare and Midway Airports. Our first mission was to deploy troops to Germany to augment security for our forces there. Amazingly, I was given a choice as to whether I should go. They only needed platoon level and below, so I didn't go. The rest of the guys either volunteered, or were "volun-told" they were going, as we say in the Army. It was a short deployment, that time, they returned home within about 6 months. By the time they returned, I was battery commander.

The US invaded Afghanistan, and my cousin Emily was a medic with the 101st Airborne, in TF Rakkasans. She was home for less than a year when George W. Bush issued orders for a "Left turn" in our war strategy and the US invaded Iraq in March 2003. She saw some serious combat in Talafar, Iraq, and was coined by General Patreaus for doing such a good job during the triage of 40 casualties. She was a specialist E-4 and had to step up and take charge, there were only three medics on duty at the time it happened. She saved lives that day. I couldn't be more proud of her. I just wish she didn't have to experience the carnage of war. By this time, I could see the handwriting on the wall, and told my guys to be ready, because our turn would be coming soon.

It was. Our military kicked ass and conquered Iraq in three weeks. But then what? Well, we were all left holding the bag while our nation's leadership tried to figure out what the hell they were doing. So we inherited the nation building business in addition to the fighting and winning the war business. It's called "mission creep." Then you have guerilla warfare combined with global terrorism and every terrorist in the world is going to Iraq to fight Americans. By the way there is still a war going on in Afghanistan, but it's not the main effort anymore. NOW we need more troops! What do we do now? We're too chicken shit to reinstate the draft, so let's call up the National Guard and Individual Ready Reservists and just use a "back door" draft instead. Plus, we can just "Stop Loss" anybody whose enlistment is about to end. Hell, it only affects 1% of the population, the US Military and their families. 99% of the people can just do nothing, and every 4 years we have another election. Then the two parties can take turns trying to get re-elected and cater to their wealthy constituents and not worry about having a long-term strategy or actually having a strategy to WIN the war. That's how you end up with our longest war in history, even longer than Vietnam! OOPS! Sorry about that, I got a little bit bitter for a minute and pissed sarcasm all over the place. Whattaya gonna do? Call me out of retirement and send me back?! Yeah, probably.

My first deployment came in 2003.

The second in 2005.

The third in 2008.

My orders came in October 2003 as I entered back into active duty. The hardest thing I ever did was throw my duffel bag up on my shoulder, kiss my crying, pregnant-three-months-with-our-second-child-wife and kiss my two and a half year old daughter goodbye while she was sleeping in her crib at 0300. I did an about-face never knowing if I would ever see them again. I took an oath to uphold and defend the Constitution of the United States, and to protect them, that's how I roll. I caught a cab in the dark and linked up with my battle buddies to O'Hare en route to Ft. Leonard-Wood, MO. As it turns out, "Big Army" decided they needed more Military Police units and didn't have enough. Some staff somewhere decided, Hey, we don't need these field artillery units in this "counter-insurgency" fight, with all that steel rain and collateral damage they cause, let's turn them into MPs! And they did. FORSCOM issued orders for 25 batteries across the country to converge on "Fort Lost in the Woods" and undergo training to Military Police Companies. The Provisional MP companies were tagged with law enforcement missions and sent to military installations across the US and overseas. My Soldiers stepped up and were squared away in a few months, ready to do our bidding. By the luck of the draw, we were tagged as Provisional MPs and sent to Germany for our mission. We replaced active duty companies in Germany with the 18th MP Brigade, in the 504th and 709th MP Battalions. My guys conducted law enforcement 24/7 for a year while those units fought in Iraq and Afghanistan. We ended up with a 6-month extension to our orders, and served for a total of 17 months before returning home. Lucky for me, my commander was generous enough to let me come home for 10 days of leave so I could be there for the birth of our second child. The lovely Miss Evelyn was born on June 10, 2004. I was there to cut the umbilical cord, change a few diapers, mow the grass; then turn around, hand a crying baby and a shocked-dazed-and-confused-3-year-old-redhead-girl-who-missed-her-Daddy back over to my wife and jet back to Germany. But we accomplished our mission keeping American families and installations overseas safe and secure.

When I returned in the spring of 2005, I was shocked at the treatment from my civilian employer. I had to fight my employer to get my job and my pay back. Which creates such extreme bitterness, that I can not even put into words. After you sacrifice and serve your country you come home to this battle. Many soldiers lost their jobs and had to start over. It was ridiculous.

Five months later, Hurricane Katrina hit New Orleans, LA. Who better to send than a recently returned Military Police unit to aid, assist, and provide security? We went again and did our job. I was happy to help our own people. But I gotta tell ya, it was eerie patrolling in an almost abandoned American city with the smell of death, garbage, no electricity, and bad water. We were a bit nervous. I drew my weapon on people a couple of times, but thankfully we didn't have to shoot anybody. It was pretty boring and sucked being away from home again. I really felt bad for some Louisiana National Guard Soldiers, who had just returned from a year of combat in Iraq, and found their homes destroyed and even lost some family members. One of the sergeants volunteered to help us with the relief effort. He went to check on his cousin because nobody could reach him. He found his body floating in the water of what remained of his home. Maybe I shouldn't complain so much, and just be thankful. I remember my last week there. I patrolled past a park, where I saw a mother pushing a little girl in a swing set. It was the most beautiful thing. People were finally starting to come back and rebuild. I thankfully returned home to my family.

I was finally ready to exhale, and breathe in my freedom, my family, and get back to normal life as best I could. I returned to teaching, which I truly enjoy. I was promoted to Major and transferred to Brigade headquarters. My wife and I renewed our wedding vows, and we tried to make the best of our life, even with the rat race and two kids to bring up. I loved them all and cherished them so much. But I had to keep one eye on the ball, and stay frosty. We were after all still fighting a war, and people were dying every day. I had to be ready. It was hard to deal with all that extra stress. It was hard on our marriage. I eventually agreed to go to marriage counseling. Unfortunately, because of the long, multiple, separations, my oldest daughter began suffering from anxiety attacks. For example, she remembered me carrying her on my back in a kid carrier while I mowed the grass. For years afterwards, she was terrified of lawn mowers, if she saw one she would scream and cry. She's also triggered by parking garages, where she remembers saying goodbye to me again, when she thought I was back for good. Even today, at 14 years old, you have to hold her hand to help her overcome her fear in a parking garage.

In January 2007, our alert orders came again. It was early on a Sunday morning at drill. I had some "guy time" with my Army buddies, Paul Meier and the "Chief," the night before. We decided to grill some steaks in the fresh January winter air, wash down a few beers, smoke cigars, and talk about the good old days, when "Chief" Loeffel breaks out a vintage bottle of whiskey and just smiles. That guy was just "scary smart!" He worked as an attorney on the civilian side, and he knew more about artillery on his little pinkie finger than I knew in 18 years of service. After a few hours of "No, shit! There I was…" stories we crashed for the night and reported for duty the next morning bright eyed and bushy tailed. The Colonel walks in the room for our morning briefing and he breaks us the good news. The guys in "State HQ" took a trip to Washington, D.C. and lobbied the National Guard Bureau at the Pentagon to pick our state for the next combat deployment, again. Assholes. It wasn't enough that many of our units already deployed to Iraq and other places multiple times. They had to have their chance, too. Playing with peoples' lives, just so they could play politics. If duty comes, fine, let's roll. That's what we signed up for. But you don't volunteer an entire Brigade of people just for your ego. "Oh, don't worry, it'll be fine. We're going to Afghanistan, not Iraq! (Big smile). And so "The Surge" in Iraq raged on as we began our year of training to prepare for war in Afghanistan in 2008. I had to go home that week and sit my wife and kids down on the couch to tell them the news. It's a touchy thing, telling your kids that you're leaving again to go to war and might not ever see them again. I chose to use a storybook to break the news this time. It was called, *The Impossible Patriotism Project* by Linda Skeers. At the end, I laminated a picture of myself in uniform, from my previous deployment, and a poem I wrote for them to read over and over again. Annie cried immediately. Evie was too young and just stared at me innocently. I had to explain it to her over again in a way she could understand. When she started to cry, I knew she finally understood. I hated making my kids cry. I hated leaving them again. But I love them, so I fight.

The next year, I felt as if the sand in an hourglass was slowly sifting away, until my time ran out. The stress gradually built up and affected my marriage even more, I was short tempered and worked all the time. Instead of one weekend a month, now I was training two or three weekends, and spent weeks and months at various training exercises traveling to Ft. McCoy, WI, Ft. Dix, NJ, Ft. Chaffee, AR, Ft. Bragg, NC, and even to California for Afghan cultural training. My wife and I went through more marriage counseling and went on a "Strong Bonds" retreat. It was supposed to draw us closer together, but she felt my traditional views were just, "unacceptable." I felt crushed, but had to keep on keeping on. The stakes were much higher now, this is not just about winning or losing a ball game, this is about life or death. I felt responsible to make sure my guys and myself were properly trained, in-shape, and ready. Now when I would finally go to combat, I would turn 40 years old and spend my 20th year in the Army in Afghanistan. That's the way it turned out for me, but I was proud to serve, and would do it again. I just wish it didn't cost so much.

I was transferred to the 1-178 Infantry Regiment as the Battalion Fire Support Officer and deployed with that unit. In August 2008, we shipped out to FT Bragg, NC where we were locked down on a mock Forward Operating Base in the field while we trained for two months. I came home on a 4 day pass to see my family one more time before I shipped out to Afghanistan in October. I cherished the days, but the grains of sand slipped through the hourglass, empty. I had to leave early on the advanced party to prepare for our Relief-in-Place. At about that time, my wife was having a nervous breakdown as the reality of everything caught up with her, and I couldn't do anything about it. Whenever I would call home or email, she would want me to talk about all the details of what was happening, but I couldn't do it. Most of the work I did was classified as SECRET at the time.

I had the job of three officers for a year in a combat zone. When we hit the ground, my forward observers were split up and sent to 12 different security platoons across the country, so each platoon could have Forward Observer capability. I had myself, four outstanding sergeants (SFC Obenauf, SFC Espinoza, SFC Comeaux, SGT Muniz) and one fine Lieutenant (1LT Nonaka) to do fire support, IO, and CMO for the entire province of Laghman in eastern Afghanistan, seven days a week, twenty-four hours a day.

As soon as we had our Relief-In-Place, everything started. First, we had a fire in the TOC (Tactical Operations Center) when one of our radios overheated. Next, I had to deal with the corruption of the Afghan Police for the first time. Some Kuchi tribesmen showed up at our front gate with 250 dead or wounded sheep and said our guys shot them and they wanted to be compensated. Simultaneously, the Afghan Police General announced to the press, confirming that we did it. It was on the internet too. I conducted an investigation and proved that we didn't. I refused to pay them and sent them away. I also had to put out IO messages telling the truth about what happened and do damage control against the enemy's propaganda, which the press simply copied and pasted! I learned pretty quickly that the enemy has an excellent propaganda machine in place, and that I couldn't necessarily trust anyone in the Afghan Police. I would later learn this to be the case for some in the Afghan National Army too. That was our first day. "Major Erwin, why did you kill all those sheep!?" Rocky, one of our interpreters would say, and all my guys would laugh.

Our mission was two fold: One, to provide security platoons (SECFOR) for each of the 12 Provisional Reconstruction Teams (PRT's) across the country. Two, was to form Task Force Bayonet and control Laghman province in RC East in cooperation with the Afghan government, Afghan National Army (ANA), Afghan National Police (ANP) and all of the enablers attached to our unit. They included: Regular Army MPs, a Field Artillery Battery, the Laghman PRT, USAID, Dynacorp and Police Trainers, both USMC and Army Embedded Training Teams (ETT's) to work with the ANP, a PSYOPS team, TF Paladin (an Explosives and Ordinance Disposal team), and two SF teams (who were under a separate chain of command).

As BN FSO, I was responsible for coordinating and providing indirect fire support in the form of mortar and artillery fire, plus coordinating air support from attack helicopters and Combat Air Support from fixed wing aircraft. I was responsible for clearing and authorizing lethal fires. I routinely did this for both mortars and artillery. I recommended to the Battalion Commander the clearance and use of air strikes, but only he had the authority to clear it. I also personally conducted calls for fire when needed. I established a need for howitzers at our Forward Operating Base (FOB Mehtar Lam), gained approval, and built a gun pit position for two 155mm howitzers, which we then utilized. SFC Obenauf, SFC Espinoza, and SGT Muniz worked to maintain our fires cell twenty-four hours a day.

As BN CMO, I was responsible for providing compensation for damage caused by ISAF (International Security and Assistance Forces). Furthermore, I was responsible for overseeing all CERP projects in Laghman province by TF Bayonet. We completed over 56 projects worth over two million dollars. I was also tasked with building another Combat Outpost (COP) in Zio Haq along Highway 1. I coordinated the necessary contracting and engineer support to build this outpost, and to help upgrade our existing COP in Najil. 1LT Nonaka and SFC Comeaux worked to help make all of that possible.

As BN IO, I was the propaganda officer for the task force. I was responsible for distributing fliers, humanitarian assistance, wanted posters, transmitting radio messages, damage mitigation, counter propaganda, news releases; both offensive and defensive Information Operations. I worked directly with our attached PSYOPS team from Texas. SGT Brian Adams, SGT Joshua Harris, and SPC Bart were outstanding. We worked together to develop customized Information Operations tailored to our area of operations and the deployment of the PSYOPS team most effectively. I also managed our combat camera SPC Lee, and later on, SGT Jason Dorsey, who both did excellent work. Towards the end of the deployment, I also was responsible for the coordination of the Afghan elections in our province with the PRT and Afghan government officials to include a presidential visit by Afghan President Hamid Karzai.

In the conduct of all my duties, I primarily operated out of FOB Mehtar Lam. What follows is a series of memories of different events during the deployment: In the fall and winter of 2008 it was relatively quiet, until the "fighting season" arrived in the spring and summer. So, one of the highlights of that November was, of course, Thanksgiving. The Army prides itself on feeding the troops, especially over the Holidays. Indeed, our logistical support was excellent. Just imagine the Herculean task of bringing a full Thanksgiving dinner with all the trimmings to every American soldier on every mountain outpost in Afghanistan all in one day. Just for our unit to get where we were, we flew from Ft. Bragg, NC to Germany, to Turkey, to Kyrgystan, and then over the Hindu Kush mountains into Bagram, Afghanistan. From there, we flew by helicopter a few hours away to Mehtar Lam, and from there, we had to push further out into the remote combat outpost. Our cooks did an outstanding job, we had one of the best "mess halls" in Afghanistan. But our guys at the combat outpost were cooking for themselves over open fire, or just eating MREs. So, by tradition, the BN commander and staff man the chow line to serve the troops; a way to honor and thank our soldiers for all they do. We served the first Thanksgiving meal to all the troops on the FOB at Mehtar Lam, then jumped on the choppers to COP Najil. The meals were flown in "mermite" insulated containers by some helo contracted to make deliveries all over the country. We set up the tactical chow line and everybody was all smiles as they had a little taste of home with all the fixings; turkey, mashed potatoes and gravy, stuffing, cranberry sauce, sweet potatoes, rolls, pie, you name it. The next morning we learned that the whole company was up all night with it coming out of both ends. They had food poisoning. By regulation, the meals delivered by mermites must be served within 4 hours. Somebody messed up. The guys laugh so hard now they want to cry. "Thanks a lot, Sir!"

Our families and the folks back home were really awesome. Care packages arrived all the time. People sent Girl Scout cookies, quilts, socks, jerky, shaving cream, batteries, coffee, DVDs; you name it. Somebody sent SFC Comeaux a bread machine! We plugged that sucker in and turned it on. The next thing you know, the smell of freshly baked bread is wafting through the Tactical Operation Center. All of a sudden, we have guys popping in to see what's going on. PSYOPS, it works!

Not all of our time there was all fun and games. Much of it sucked. "Embrace the suck!" was one of our favorite sayings. I had the displeasure of dealing with the fallout of two operations by Special Operations Forces in our area, which left 47 Afghans KIA. One took place in December 2008 and another in January 2009 in the vicinity of Masamute Bala and Galuch villages. The strike teams wait until the conditions are right for taking out a High Value Target (HVT) based on intel reports, radio chatter, cell phone calls, human intelligence, patterns of life, etc. They successfully took out the HVTs in our area of operations, but when an Afghan village is attacked at night, everybody there fights back. Some of the

KIA were definitely Taliban, but some were locals. The end result was the SF teams did their hit and run, took out the HVTs, and were gone by morning. But our Task Force had to deal with the hostility from the locals. Overnight, we had angry crowds throwing rocks at us, and at the Afghan governor, who like any "good politician" quickly threw us under the bus. We had a huge increase in IEDs and attacks against our Task Force in the weeks that followed until things quieted back down to "normal" again. The enemy propaganda painted an ugly picture of half-truths and outright lies all over the press.

On March 15, 2009, one of our vehicles hit an IED that killed four men onboard while they were checking on a school project in Nangarhar. The 4 KIAs were SGT Christopher P. Abeyta, SPC Robert M. Weinger, SPC Norman Cain III, and SSGT Timothy Bowles (USAF). Later, on May 10, 2009, SGT Lukasz Saczek died in a "non-combat related" incident. We also suffered 12 wounded in action during the deployment. One of them was one of my forward observers, SPC Steele. He was attached to the PRT in Nuristan province at FOB Kalagush. I made several trips there without incident, but I still feel guilty for his injuries. An IED flipped his vehicle over, and he was the gunner in the turret. He managed to duck down to survive, but it completely broke his legs and hips. He required multiple surgeries and finally came home to Chicago from Walter Reed Hospital about a year after the rest of us were already home. I saw it on the local news. By April 2009, I began to worry if I would make it home myself, or if I would be wounded also. It could just have easily been me, or any of my other soldiers who could be blown up by an IED in a HMMWV and get killed. My hands began to shake, but I hid this from everyone and just kept doing my job as best I could.

On June 3, 2009, I was involved in a Troops In Contact (TIC) at FOB Mehtar Lam when we received small arms fire and Rocket Propelled Grenade (RPG) fire. I assumed my role as FSO and directed mortar fire against the enemy and coordinated air support while our Quick Reaction Force (QRF) responded and pursued the enemy. That night, I later found out that one of our mortar illumination rounds landed near a house in Mehtar Lam, injuring a woman. I was responsible for that action since I cleared the fires. The imagery we used to clear fires was out of date, and more homes had been built since then. So it looked clear, but wasn't. So we updated our imagery to clear fires with at that point.

I regularly made trips to our Combat Outpost in Najil and to our new combat outpost in Zio Haq. I was involved in several TICs at the Combat

Outpost in Najil, where we were attacked most often. One in particular involved the attempted assassination of one of our Afghan contractors, Lol Mohammed. The Taliban dressed in all white "man jammies" approached him in the village market of Najil just adjacent to our combat outpost and ambushed him in broad daylight. He was wounded and fled to our outpost. I was there at the medic shack when he arrived, with his bone sticking out of his leg, while he was moaning and bleeding, but relatively calm. I let the Doc (1LT Hutchison) and medics do their work and got out of their way. Nobody wants some pain-in-the-ass-major getting in the way and making them nervous. He needed to be evacuated so I made myself useful by contacting higher HQ and requesting approval from the BN Commander on up the chain of command to have him evacuated by MEDEVAC helicopter. This is usually not done for Afghan Nationals, but we made a special request since he was one of our contractors. It was approved. It saved his life, and he was able to continue doing work for us in the area. Meanwhile, the American QRF, ANA, and ASG (Afghan Security Guards, who were related to Lol Mohammed) led a counterattack to pursue the Taliban up the side of the mountain towards the "V-Notch", one of our Target Reference Points. I held back from calling a fire mission and ordering our .50 caliber machine guns to open up. I let CPT Gosnell, the Company Commander, run the show. We didn't want to hit any of our guys or the friendly Afghans engaged in the firefight as they pursued up the mountain. They killed one of the Taliban and brought his body back to the COP. I was there when they brought him in. It was my first body. He was dressed in all white, with a full beard, long black hair, and wore tennis shoes for climbing the mountains. He had bullet-hole entrance wounds in his chest with exit wounds in his back. I mostly remember his face, with his eyes wide open, and his teeth showing, almost like he was smiling. He looked like Jesus, which really stood out to me, and would visit me later in my dreams, but not until I got back home.

Another time, I was staying with my Mortar Platoon when we were hit at night. It woke me up and I jumped up, threw on my gear, locked and loaded, and ran out into the mortar pit with the rest of the platoon. COP Najil was regularly hit with 107mm rockets, 82mm mortars, crew served machine gun fire, RPGs, and small arms fire. I assisted the platoon by sometimes acting as FO to do calls for fire, and other times clearing fires with the Fire Direction Center (FDC) as we fired 120mm mortars at the enemy. I also did my fair share by pulling guard duty in the guard towers and by going on a few foot patrols and mounted patrols with the infantry platoons out of COP. They liked it when I was there to clear fires, because it happened a lot faster with me there instead of calling up to Battalion. SFC Kevin Driscoll and his guys did a kick ass job of laying into the enemy using "Shake and Bake" HE and WP rounds to make the Taliban pay whenever they chose to attack us. However, on one occasion when I was awakened in the middle of the night and asked to clear fires, I feel like I disappointed my men. They asked me to clear an 81mm mission in support of a patrol in the Mayl valley. They saw two Afghans hiding behind rocks in the distance about 0300 hours at night. It was my call, but I denied the mission because they couldn't see any weapons, then they got away. My guys were pissed off at me for not clearing it. Maybe I was wrong, but I had to be sure it was the enemy. Today, I feel like I let them down, and regret the decision, but it helps me to understand how my commander, LTC Dan Fuhr (who I admire and respect), must have felt whenever he was called upon to decide if someone will live or die that day.

On a few other occasions, local nationals would bring their kids to the medics asking for help. Policy was that we are supposed to turn them away. But, for God's sake, they're kids. So we helped them whenever we could. We gave them candy, stuffed animals, things people sent from home. Unfortunately, a few of the kids were burned. It wasn't our fault, but we treated them. As a father, the image of those kids with burns on their legs and in pain bothered me, but at least we helped them.

One day, in the Qargayee district in the south, one of our patrols was driving north when an Afghan civilian vehicle containing a family, pulled out in front of one of our big Mine Resistant Armor Protected (MRAP) vehicles. The MRAP couldn't stop in time and crashed into the civilian vehicle, killing the family. One of our medics jumped out and tried to help, but the local Afghans nearby became enraged and wouldn't let him touch them. The local police showed up and dragged away the bodies. That night, I Skyped with my wife, she wanted me to tell her what's going on. How could I? "Well, Honey, There was a terrible accident and we accidentally killed a family today…" I couldn't do it.

We had 5 battalion operations called Operation Longbow that took us way out into western Mehtar Lam district in an area know as the Galuch Valley. The previous year while we were training at FT Bragg, NC, we heard intel that 10 French soldiers were killed there, and their bodies were mutilated. I personally went on two of those missions as the Forward Observer. I will not ask any of my men to do anything that I would not do myself. Whenever we did this, we had to pull 12 hour shifts in the fire support cell in the TOC because we did not have enough forward observers. We took turns doing it. There is only one way in and one way out of the Galuch Valley, and the enemy knows it. It was about 28 kilometers one way through the mountains, and at the very edge of our artillery range. We had to plan the use of rocket assisted projectiles to reach that far. We also took our 81mm mortars with us, and planned CAS sorties to support it too. The first mission was uneventful, until the way back. A pressure plate IED with three 122mm artillery rounds was buried in the road. Seven of our vehicles drove over it before my PSYOPS team spotted it. Luckily, it did not go off. That was a close call. We spotted two Afghan nationals fleeing on a motorcycle. With the help of the ANA, we captured them for questioning and they were put into Afghan custody. For another Longbow mission, I stayed in the TOC to clear fires while my NCO went as the FO.

On the next one, I went again as the FO. This time the plan was to stay overnight. I brought SPC Eagan with me and a laser designator. When we set up in the Galuch valley, we were in a huge bowl, surrounded by mountains on all sides. The BN Commander, ANA Commander, and PRT Commander all were in a face to face Key Leader Engagement with the local leaders while we pulled security and set up our positions. It was an eerie feeling because when we looked up, we could see several Afghan figures standing on top of the mountain watching our every move. SPC Eagan and I targeted them for a mortar mission and stood by to call it in. According to our Rules of Engagement (ROE), we needed positive ID of the enemy; and see a weapon. They were too far away to see any weapons, even with the laser designator, so we just waited to see if we received fire. It was creepy knowing that we were being watched and couldn't do anything about it. I also arranged for a sling load of humanitarian assistance to give to the local village elders. It was a 5,500 pound load of rice, wheat, beans, cooking oil, PSYOP fliers, and radios. All of these were popular items with the Afghans. The Chinook helicopter accidentally released the sling load too early, about 100 feet up. It fell on the ground and smashed. Luckily none of our guys were crushed. The Afghans scurried to pick up the food, even the grains of rice that spilled into the dirt, they didn't care. When we set up for the night, we started digging in our positions, but the ground was too rocky to do any good. We worked out a rotation to take turns using the laser designator with its night vision capability. In the middle of the night, the Brigade Commander made the call for us to return to the FOB immediately instead of waiting in place overnight. He may have had intel from radio chatter and UAV feeds. He was worried that the enemy had too much time to react and set up an ambush on our way out; which is back the same way we came in. So we hastily march ordered and started our return trip through the dangerous mountain passes at night. It was tricky driving. He arranged for OH-58 Kiowa Warrior helicopters and AH-64 Apache helicopters to cover us on our way out. They were zig-zagging above us the whole way out. I was waiting to hit an IED, but amazingly we made it! I got back to the FOB around 0330 hours and fell straight to sleep.

Up to that point, we had a hard time getting attack aircraft when we needed them because they were usually further east in Kunar province, Nangarhar province, or up north in Nuristan. SFC Obenaurf arranged to set up a Forward Area Rearm Refuel Point (FARP) at our LZ. This made it a lot easier to reach out to them whenever they came to our location to rearm and refuel. "Hey, buddy, would you mind swinging by COP Najil on your way?" One time I went for a jog around the LZ to get some exercise right when an Apache was taking off. Jet exhaust knocked me over as it took off. Those are some powerful birds! I grew to enjoy seeing the OH-58's flying overhead of my convoys. I would later have dreams about the OH-58 gunships flying over-head. Their call sign was "Pale Horse."

We had another incident at COP Najil. I was the investigating officer. One of the SOF teams traveled there to kick off an operation in a village nearby to go after one of our HVT's in the Mayl Valley. This was the third time. Each time, somehow the enemy knew they were coming and they would be ambushed. They suspected that an ANA soldier or interpreter was spying and warning the enemy. The team was on the COP giving their mission briefing before rolling out. They noticed an Afghan soldier standing nearby talking on his cell phone. They told him, through an interpreter to stop, and to get away. But he refused and was uncooperative. They decided to force him. One Soldier brought him down and zip tied him, while the other pulled out his pistol and covered his partner. Immediately, when the other Afghan soldiers saw this happen the situation escalated dangerously. The Afghan commander ordered all of his men to lock and load, and they pointed their weapons at all US Soldiers on the COP, including crew served weapons. Our guys locked and loaded too. It was a very hairy moment. All it took was one undisciplined guy and we would have a company sized friendly fire incident on the outpost! These were the Afghans that we lived and served with everyday for the whole deployment. CPT Gosnell, the

US Company Commander ran up and talked to the ANA Company commander and de-escalated the situation, both sides stood down. For quite a while thereafter, there was a lack of trust. Soldiers carried their M4s with them all the time and were on edge. I was worried too. We shared our FOB and our outposts with Afghan National Army and Afghan Security Guards, the enemy could somehow infiltrate their ranks and turn on us at any time. This made the last few months of the deployment even more stressful. Luckily, we had a very close relationship with the ANA Battalion commander. He relieved the hot-headed ANA Company commander and the SOF team relocated.

There was another TIC that took place on July 4, 2009. I remember it because we had planned a "Forward Observer Training" for midnight that night to celebrate July 4th. Amazingly, the enemy was stupid enough to attack us that night; we already had the ammo set aside and ready to use and targets picked out. So we let them have it when they attacked us that night! I ended up doing one of the calls for fire that night, adjusting the 155mm artillery rounds for the commander at COP Najil. I found out the next day from our intel; one of our informants confirmed that we killed two Taliban on the backside of the mountain with indirect fire. I signed off on a sworn statement for the soldiers of Alpha Battery, 1-6 FA for their Combat Action Badges that night.

At night, we got to the point where we were able to pattern what was going to happen, we just couldn't know for sure where or when. When there was a full moon, there would be an attack at COP Najil up north in the mountains. The Taliban preferred climbing the mountains at night with a little moonlight to lead the way. Without a full moon it would be completely black at night, so they would prefer to lay ambushes at night along Highway 1. It's easier to get in close, pop up and spray some AK-47, PKM machine gun fire, and RPG's... and then disappear in the darkness before the QRF comes. Or they would hit COP Zio Haq - the Combat Out Post we built to secure the main supply route along Highway 1. After they attacked it a few times too many, we sent patrols up into the mountains to clear out the caves. Hump up into the mountainside. Send somebody into the cave. Set up the butt load of C-4, run back out and set off the Det cord. Problem solved.

A good way to pass the time was to work out. My "Battle Buddy" and partner in crime was MAJ Paul Edwards, our BN Intel officer. We were both pretty busy, but made time to link up at zero dark thirty in the morning to lift weights and go for a run around the FOB to stay in shape. Our deal was that if

I got shot, he would carry me out, and that if he was shot, I would carry him out, plus we were both trying to "bring sexy back" by being so buff. We would both laugh it off and make fun of MAJ Hible for being bald but still the sexiest guy on the FOB. We're all still friends today. Each day of the week had it's own name. "Malaria Monday" as a reminder to take your malaria pills, Mefloquine. "Two-fer Tuesday," "Wacky-Wednesday." "Man-Love Thursday." "Freaky-Friday." "Same-Sex Saturday," and "Same-Sex Sunday" each had their own frustrated sexual connotations. As you could tell, we really missed our wives. After working twenty-four hours a day, seven days a week, for a year, without R&R, we were ready to come home!

We were scheduled for our Relief-In-Place in late July 2009. We had a plan in place for our replacements, but we had to scrap it due to the situation on the ground. The enemy gets a vote. We sent a patrol into the Mayl valley to check on the Tili village school project I started there. The Pashtun locals in this area wore black beards, often with a red dye or henna mixed in, and what looked to us like black eye liner under their eyes. It gave them an almost devil-like appearance. It was a dangerous area. Against my advice, we sent in a mix of MRAP vehicles and HMMWVs on that patrol. Having been there before, I knew that the road into this valley was very primitive and narrow, and would not support the heavy MRAPs. Also, it was yet another situation of only one way in and one way out. But the higher command HQ put out a decree that at least two MRAPs must go on every patrol, because we were taking higher casualties due to IEDs. Sure enough, on the way out, the enemy hit them with a complex ambush of IEDs, RPGs, and small arms fire. We cleared the IED, responded to the enemy ambush with direct fire, indirect fire, and air support, then began to exfil. However, the edge of the narrow road collapsed and an MRAP vehicle rolled over and went down into the Mayl valley along the riverbed. Luckily, the crew evacuated before it finally flipped over. These vehicles weigh near 30 tons, so it could not be pulled out, and it could not be airlifted out by Chinook helicopter either. The engineering of the V-shaped hull of these vehicles was classified at the time, and had not yet been defeated by enemy IED makers... So now we had a high priority situation on our hands. So for the new unit, this operation became their on-the-job-training for the Relief-In-Place. The patrol tossed in Thermite grenades to try to burn up the vehicle and destroy it in place. It burned all night, and we had to rotate platoons in to hold the position overnight. The most amazing thing happened, when the enemy attacked from deep in the Mayl Valley, the villagers from Tili fought back against them! The school project and other efforts helped to gain their support. But the MRAP was still intact even after burning all night. So we called in support from Brigade HQ. They flew in a welder to try to cut it apart so we could pull out the classified stuff, but it didn't work. In the meantime, our EOD guys came up with a plan they proposed to our BN Commander. They said they would daisy chain three 155mm shells and wrap it with C-4 then blow it up. He asked, "Are you sure this will work?" and they said, "Well, Sir, we think so." He shot it down. Then we flew in an explosives expert from Division. He was able to use plastic explosives to make "surgical cuts" to the hull piece by piece. It took him an entire day while we continued to pull security. We evacuated the local villagers who were in the danger zone. The next day we were able to hook the crucial pieces to a cable and haul them out. Then we had to compensate the villagers for the damages. Although very stressful, it was also very satisfying because of the support we had from the locals in the valley after working hard to make progress for a year.

We began ramping up our preparations for the upcoming elections when Karzai ended up getting re-elected after we went home. It had to be Afghan led, but they really needed our logistical support. We had 128 election sites to secure in the province. We ended up helping the Afghans to register 196,000 Afghans to vote. I was proud of that. There would later be accusations of corruption during the election, which doesn't surprise me, but at least they were able to vote. By the end of our deployment, we had over 150 engagements with the enemy, destroyed over $120,000 worth of munitions, planned or completed over 56 projects valued at $2.7 million dollars which included 4 schools, 16 school walls, 2 bridges, 34 wells or pipe schemes, and road improvements. The last thing I did before leaving was to put a daily Bible study book that someone left for me in the drawer of my hootch for my replacement. I used it to pray every morning, not knowing if that would be my last day. I knew he would need it.

The Laghman PRT planned or implemented larger scale projects. We worked our butts off to support the counter-insurgency effort of improved governance, improved security, economic development, and information operations about improving life in Laghman province. It would later be one of the first provinces to go under Afghan control in Mehtar Lam in 2011, but not without casualties. When I got home, I later found out the mayor of Mehtar Lam was assassinated by a suicide bomber. I used to sit right next to him at the Governor's compound when we held coordination meetings. When it happened, one of my Afghan contractors, Hajji Guncha Gul, was wounded by shrapnel in the face. Luckily, he survived. I also watched the security tape when a car bomb went off in Nangarhar at FOB Fenty in Jalalabad. A group of school kids were walking home from school right past the gate when the enemy detonated the VBIED. I'm a teacher back home, so that really bothered me.

We finished up our Relief-In-Place and began our exfil to Bagram for our ticket that would eventually take us back home. We would eventually go from there to Kyrgystan, then Germany, FT Dix, NJ, and then back to FT McCoy, WI, before finally being demobilized and sent back home to "Fort Living Room." My replacement CMO later sent me pictures the following January showing the completion of the Tili school project and the passing out of school supplies to the kids, plus the construction of four other schools I started before I left. It was very satisfying to see these accomplishments come to fruition. In the years after our rotation, the situation worsened in Afghanistan, with other units rotating in to each fight their own "one-year-war." I often wonder what will happen to those kids, the teachers, interpreters, contractors, and those in the Afghan government who worked closely with us as we pulled out. This was especially true in light of the "WikiLeaks" situation, in which all of that secret information of who we worked with, when, and where, was incomprehensibly released!

I chose to retire in 2010 after 21 years of service. I was awarded a bronze star, meritorious service medal and a letter of commendation from COMISAF. However, my reintegration did not go well. We finally came home on August 3, 2009, just three weeks short of a year for the deployment. I was actually on leave until October 17, 2009, but went back to work when school started in August. I knew my employer would just dock my pay again if I didn't start on time. I was really happy to be home and back with my family. I felt like I just ran a marathon and finally made it across the finish line. We had a nice welcome home party, yellow ribbons, police escort, Freedom Riders on motorcycles and everything. It was nice to see my wife and kids again. We even went to Disney World. But little did I know that the bottom was going to drop out from underneath me. I really didn't have time to decompress.

My first nightmare was on my first night back home. The dreams were quite vivid and real. In my dream, I was in Afghanistan and the OH-58 helicopter gunships came in to support us. But this time, every time I moved, the gunship would follow me. "Pale Horse" was always my friend, but this time it was pointing its weapons at me. It came in close, so I could see the pilot, but his face was completely blank, no eyes, no nose, no lips; just a blank face. Then he let loose and fired at me. But then the face morphed into a devil's head. He was laughing at me. I came home without a scratch, but he said, "I wasn't allowed to lay a hand on you for an entire year. I kept my promise; but now I can go after your family!" I woke up and jumped out of bed, ran to the bathroom and started dry-heaving. (Before I left for the deployment, my church all laid hands on me and prayed that I would come home safe. Thankfully, I did). My wife asked if I was OK, but I wasn't. Later on, when I had the dream again, the pilot's face turned into her face, and I couldn't understand why. And so began my journey with PTSD.

Another time, I was sitting in the living room eating breakfast and watching TV with my family on a Saturday morning. The kids were watching an old episode of "Bewitched." It was around Halloween. One of the characters had on a monster mask, with big white teeth protruding out, I immediately started crying and breathing heavily as a panic attack set in. It reminded me of the face of the dead Taliban I saw up close, with his teeth showing like he was smiling.

If I knew something was coming, I would be OK with it, like fireworks on July 4th. But I would talk about how it reminded me of the fire missions with the 120mm mortars and shooting the 155mm howitzers with family and friends, and they would just look at me like I was from the moon. However, if I didn't know it was coming and it surprised me, then it would freak me out. Our local minor league baseball team sets off fireworks after their Friday night games, and we live close by. So sometimes I would forget, and it would make me jumpy when it started. I would make sure the house was locked up, and that my family was safe and secure. I also found that when I watched a movie or documentary about Afghanistan or Iraq that I would likely have dreams that night. But at the same time, I'm very interested in what's happening over there and very proud but I get pissed off because people over here act like nothing is happening.

My wife and I had a huge argument and she told me that she wanted a divorce. We had gone to counseling almost immediately after I came home, because I wanted to fix things and make it right as soon as possible. I thought everything was going to be okay until then. My wife and kids meant everything to me, that is why I put my life on the line and sacrificed all these years, for them. But then to have all that taken away from me after 19 years together hit me to the core. I found a note from my wife saying she loved someone else. I just lost it. I couldn't hold it together anymore. I knew I needed help. I had drill that night and reported for duty the next day. I told my battalion commander that I just couldn't lead troops anymore, I was broken and needed to see a Chaplain. He was very understanding and supportive. He arranged for me to see the Chaplain right away. He helped me and also followed up with me. I sought counseling and my doctor prescribed some medication to help me calm down. The counseling helped in the long run, but it was a struggle. I cried almost every day, suffered from anxiety and depression, and could hardly sleep for 9 months. I needed love and acceptance from my wife and kids. My daughter walked up to me one day and said, "I love you, Daddy" right out of the blue. I held her little kindergarten body in my arms and looked into her innocent eyes and said to myself, "I've got to hold on." That helped a lot. It was difficult, my wife felt bitterness and resentment towards me, and I felt rejected by her when I needed most to be forgiven, loved, and accepted. When I was finally home, after being on the other side of the world in a combat zone wanting more than anything to be home with my wife and kids, I was sitting right next to her and she didn't want me anymore. It was daily torture. Now I knew why people volunteered to turn around and go back to Afghanistan.

But I wanted a happy ending. So I gave the counseling everything I had. I turned to my faith and did my best to convince my wife to take me back. I did The Love Dare and continued with counseling. I submitted my letter of retirement, and officially retired on June 13, 2010 with 21 years of service. My wife and I took a vacation to Canada. Thankfully, my wife changed her mind about the divorce, and I felt more like myself in the latter part 2011. As the US killed Osama Bin Laden on May 2, 2011, I started getting involved in veteran's activities both to help myself and to help others.

One day I went out to lunch with a WW II Veteran and a dear friend of mine, Col. Dave Olson. He knew first hand what I was going through, and offered me sound advice. "Jack, you need to find many joys in life, so that if you lose one, you have another to take its place."

I found that physical fitness helped relieve stress and keep my mind in the present. I joined the Wounded Warrior Project and started training to run my first marathon in 2012. I was a soldier, a leader, a warrior, but now, I felt like I was nothing. Being a Wounded Warrior "Alumni" helped to give me an identity again. I called up Sgt. Steele, my soldier who had lost his leg to an IED, and told him I was running it for him. I think we both cried over the phone. He thanked me and I promised him I wouldn't quit, that I would make it to the finish line. I did. I also did it to show my wife that I wasn't going to give up, that I would be in it for the long run. I raised about $3,200 for WWP and finished in 4 hours and 53 minutes. My daughter ran the last 100 yards with me to the finish line. My buddy, and former soldier, Sgt. Jason Dorsey was there as a photographer. When I came across the finish line, we both hugged and cried. He joined me for the TOUGH MUDDER too, when I was sponsored by WWP in 2013.

I also found writing about my war experience to have an amazing therapeutic quality to it. If you can somehow put it on paper and tell your story, there is a healing quality to it. That brings us to the Line of Advance. While deployed, our unit was given a line of advance, a military term for which we were to go no farther. If you did, you would be going deeper into the valley than you were authorized to go, beyond where the road ends and you can only continue on foot, but there is no guarantee that you will ever make it back. You were living on the edge. There are many places like this in Afghanistan. I am extremely proud to say that upon our return, several of my soldiers took the initiative to launch a website for veteran writers. It's called www.lineofadvance.org It was launched by Sgt. Chris Lyke, Spc. Matt Marcus, and Lt. Ryan Quinn. They spearheaded the project, raised the money, and launched the site. It was dedicated as a venue for us to write about our experiences however the writer chooses, writings were collected and certain writings were selected to be published in quarterly journals. I was honored to write several blogs for them. (*"The Welcome"* and *"The Long Walk & the Search for the Holy Grail"* in 2013 and *"Warriors on the Hunt"* and *"Battle Scars, Boots, Hooves & A Healing Place"* in 2014). I was even more thrilled when my work of fiction entitled, *"In the Blackness of the Night"* was published in Journal Volume 2 in 2014.

But there is still more to be done. We lose over 22 veterans per day. I've personally known three. If you would truly like to understand what's going on with them, do your homework. There are several books that I would recommend; they are *The Long Walk: a Story of War and the Life that Follows* by Brian Castner, Matterhorn and *What It Is Like To Go To War* by Carl Merlantes, and *Tears of A Warrior* by Janet and Anthony Seahorn. This is especially true if you are a family member of a veteran, friend, or a professional caregiver of a veteran.

In 2014, my wife changed her mind again, and we ended our 23-year relationship by getting divorced. I was crushed. Someone reached out to me and invited me on an equestrian therapy retreat for veterans. Horses have an amazing ability to connect with people emotionally; it is a part of their survival instinct. I learned much more at this program than just about horses. I learned that real everyday people do actually care, and they are willing to volunteer their time, their horse, their ear, or whatever they can, to show thanks for their freedom at a personal level. It is a 5 day program, fully funded by the organization and no cost to the veteran and their family. In the morning session we work with horses and in the afternoon session there are group and art therapy programs. Everyday we shared meals, stories, and kinship. This is where I met Jordan Holwell, the brain trust behind this book, Samantha Barnard LMT, Dr. Leona Di Amore, Mitch and Larissa Tyler, Shane Wilkinson, Jeff Bourque and his wife; all of who are amazing people. The program is called "Hope and Promise" in Maple Park, IL. Another excellent program is "Bravehearts" in Harvard, IL.

One day, right after my divorce, I ventured out for a 10K run to blow off some steam. I was keeping a promise to someone I met at Hope and Promise, who also volunteered her time at this race to fundraise for families of cancer survivors. The person standing next to me ended up running with me the whole way, as we were talking, she introduced me to "Team Red, White, & Blue" a group dedicated to enriching the lives of veterans through physical and social activities and building relationships. I checked it out online at www.teamrwb.org and joined. I have since met so many amazing people and just clicked with lots of other veterans just like me, creating new friendships and reconnecting with old ones. Since then, I've had a lot of fun trying new things. I did another TOUGH MUDDER as part of Team RWB, attended yoga camp and now do Bikram Yoga, joined a cycling group, and a CrossFit gym, started to learn rowing, and now I am an area leader for Team RWB. As one thing led to another, I joined a veterans cycling group called "Ride2Recovery" and now have a road bike they donated to me! I used it to complete my first 100 mile century, and also participated in their Barrington Honor Ride and Chicago Honor Ride. I'm also in the American Legion, VFW, and IAVA.

PTSD can rob you of your sleep, your sense of safety and normalcy, and can contribute to destroying relationships with those whom you love. But there's more. There is also the survivor's guilt, and that overwhelming sense of the loss of your own humanity and moral identity. You can get angry with God, and feel completely overwhelmed. You may feel like you are drowning, I will reach out and offer you my hand – grab it! "You need to find many joys in life." God loves you! You can heal and find hope. Over time, I've gradually learned that it is OK to love again. You will too.

I am forever grateful to have had both the honor and privilege of leading American soldiers. Hopefully, sharing my story can help other soldiers who struggle with the same issues when they come home. A great way to help yourself is by helping others. ✧

Jack Erwin is now retired from the Army National Guard after 21 years, including 3 deployments. Jack commanded a battery of artillerymen who served as Military Police from 2003 to 2005. Shortly after returning home, he deployed for Hurricane Katrina in New Orleans, LA in 2005. He served in Afghanistan from 2008-2009 with the 1-178 IN under TF Duke. Shortly after returning home, Jack struggled with a difficult reintegration with his family and was eventually diagnosed with PTSD, retired in 2010. He works as a teacher in Illinois and is active in veterans' groups such as Team Red, White and Blue, the Wounded Warrior Project, and Line of Advance. ✦

john.erwin@cusd200.org

jjerwin2000@yahoo.com

Adam Kinosh

I wanted to be Rambo when I grew up.

I may have told people that I wanted to be an athlete or a rock star or something; but I would've been lying to them. I wanted to be a badass warrior, just like something straight out of a movie. I wanted to go into battle and test myself against armed enemy combatants for the thrill… and because I honestly believed I would be good at it.

I am an adrenaline junkie and I have craved adventure and passion and excitement my entire life. I grew up watching Stallone, Schwarzenegger, and Segal movies and listening to heavy metal and gangsta rap. My great uncle, John Czarnowski, who fought on Okinawa in 1945, told me a war story one night when I was 15 years old that scared the shit out of me and cemented my life's direction at the same time.

Chasing this dream would end up being one of the greatest adventures of my entire life! But it came with a cost that I wasn't fully prepared for.

By my senior year in high school, I had made up my mind that I would join the Marines upon graduation. I didn't know a whole lot about the military; there were only a few people in my family who ever served. It was 1999 and there was no war going on, but I did know that if I wanted to find combat, the Marines would be a good place to start. They had a reputation for toughness and a long, victorious battle lineage.

But if I'm being completely honest, I never really considered myself a Marine at all. The U.S. Government kind of has the monopoly on violence. So I put up with the rules and regulations, and did the dick dancing and ate all the shit sandwiches for 14 years, simply for the opportunity to be a professional gunfighter and play on the field of battle.

I grew up in northwest Connecticut, which was (and still is) a very boring place for an explorer like myself. I played community youth sports when I was young, and I raced BMX bikes on a national level as a teenager. My parents had divorced when I was three; my mother, Diana, worked her ass off so that my younger brother, Jason, and I could have the best life possible. She did an amazing job. However, that meant that she was never home, and so my grandparents Mimi and Boompa effectively raised us.

But, in many aspects, I feel like I had to figure life out on my own. Our father, John, legally had unlimited visitation rights, but chose to see us on a limited basis, yet we had a somewhat healthy relationship with him when we were young. Boompa died from aggressive cancer when I was 12 and after, as we got older, our father began to slip back into a lifestyle of booze and drugs that ultimately claimed his life in 2000 at the age of 46. I was 18 years old.

At that point, I'd just started my Marine Corps career at Parris Island, SC, on July 19, 1999. I actually did very well in boot camp and earned a meritorious promotion from Private to Private First Class upon graduation. I was even interviewed for the Marine Corps' highly selective Yankee White program, which would have put me in a position of working with the President. But as soon as they realized I had tattoos, I was sent back to doing pushups. High-fiving the President sounded cool; but shooting bad guys in the face sounded better to me anyway.

After boot leave I went straight to the School of Infantry (SOI) in North Carolina, and spent the first couple years of my enlistment as an infantry rifleman. Deployments were hard to come by at that time, but I was fortunate enough to be able to deploy with the 22nd Marine Expeditionary Unit (MEU) to the Mediterranean Sea aboard the USS Portland in late 2000.

It was on this deployment that I experienced the loss of a Marine brother for the first time.

One of my platoonmates, Corporal Franco, fell 30 feet from a catwalk in the well deck of the ship and struck his head on an armored amphibious vehicle below. He fell into a coma and died a few days later at a hospital in Germany. We had a memorial on the ship a few days after Franco died, then continued on with the rest of the deployment. It was strange for me to quickly become accustomed to the condensed grieving process that is necessary for survival in the warrior subculture.

Over the years, more of these initial platoonmates of mine would die. Mustafa Byrd fell asleep driving and died in a roll over. Big Ron Payne would fall in battle against the Taliban in Afghanistan. And Bruce Antis would join them some years later. These were some of the best men I have ever known, and we cut our teeth together as Marines. I had no idea how many friends we would all end up losing over the next decade and a half.

After about two years in the Grunts, I decided to challenge myself yet again and try out for the Marine Corps Reconnaissance community. It seemed like a natural progression for me. I had learned a great deal in the infantry and now I felt like I was ready for a momentous challenge! Recon Marines are the next level, they are sent into battle in small teams, forward of the main forces, in order to spy on the enemy, wreak havoc and mayhem, and keep the commanders informed of the enemy situation and disposition. They attended advanced training such as parachuting, scuba diving, sniper training… and they had tons of high-tech gadgets and weapons! The Navy has the SEALs, the Army has the Green Berets and Rangers and the Marine Corps has Recon.

I couldn't help it – I was pulled in that direction, and on May 5th, 2001, on a Naval base in southern Spain, I ended up being the only Marine from my ship to try out and pass the grueling physical selection known as the Recon Indoc. But that was only the beginning.

A few short months later, I was reporting to Amphibious Reconnaissance School (ARS) in Virginia Beach, VA, for an opportunity to earn the title of Recon Marine. 9/11 had just happened and we knew we were headed to war. I knew that if I didn't pass this course, I would be sent back to the grunts — and I wanted to fight alongside the best, so failure simply wasn't an option for me.

ARS is to this day still the most physically demanding course I have ever attended in my life. This 12-week gut check is meant to weed out the weak and evaluate the rest. The attrition rate was close to 50% and after my second attempt (due to a wicked back injury); I earned the title of Recon Marine. Everyone was 20 pounds lighter and limping at graduation; but we were proud.

This is where I first met a man by the name of Captain Douglas Zembiec. We had learned about him when I was attending a 4-month Recon Indoctrination Program to prepare us for Recon school. He was serving as the executive officer in charge of ARS and he essentially taught us how to be warriors. He was one of the greatest mentors I've ever had, and one of the greatest warriors of our generation. 6 foot 4 and solid muscle, he would run us to death up and down the beach and a giant monster mountain of sand known as "Loch Ness." He kept us focused and motivated as he spoke of Valhalla and battle and glory. He was a true warrior and a natural leader, and I feel very fortunate to have known him.

However, being evaluated by this man was certainly one of the most stressful things I've ever had to do in my life. A few years later Doug would become known as "The Lion of Fallujah" for his battlefield accolades during the battle of Fallujah. I don't think anyone was surprised; we were just even prouder to know him. However on May 11, 2007, Major Douglas Zembiec would fall from enemy machine gun fire in an ambush near Baghdad while working for the CIA's Special Activities Division, Ground Branch. His journey as a warrior had led him to be selected for one of the most elite military exchange programs in the world. His legacy still inspires all U.S. Marines to this day.

Following graduation from Recon school, I ended up being assigned to 2nd Reconnaissance Battalion at Camp Lejeune, NC. I spent about five years at that command learning as much as I could. I am proud to say I was able to help recruit and train approximately 100 Recon candidates in that short time, and some of them are still running and gunning down bad guys to this day! I've told them of Douglas Zembiec and tried to impart as much of his warrior ethos into training as possible.

In 2004 I met a woman named Jennifer and we fell in love. We were young and crazy and we got married after dating just six months. It was nice to have someone to come home to after work and someone to go on adventures with. But I was definitely a terrible husband. I was a selfish drunk who was out all the time partying with my friends and strippers until whenever. My heart was always really with the teams, and I couldn't wait to get back to work.

I prepared for my opportunity to deploy to combat and eventually I lead a Recon team in Iraq in 2005-2006. The deployment was difficult, dealing with everything from poor intelligence to religion, politics, saturation of forces, incredibly incompetent assholes, poor leadership, lots of mortar attacks, IEDs, and suicide bombings.

My Recon platoon came home relatively unscathed. But I lost many friends in adjacent platoons as the Iraq war raged on, and that was always difficult to deal with. But I didn't deal with it honestly; I had become so accustomed to ignoring my emotions, numbing with drinking, and moving on to the next thing all too quickly instead of facing it. This was where the drinking really started to get out of control, which was an all-too-common reality for many of us. Self-medication seemed normal and even natural, when every year, we were losing more and more friends to a war with no end in sight.

The day I returned from Iraq in May 2006, we found out that we had lost another friend and one of my former students, Cory Palmer. So instead of going on post-deployment leave, a bunch of us loaded up into cars and drove to Delaware for Cory's funeral. I remember walking up the street to the church in our dress-blue uniforms. It was a beautiful day, and there was an enormous American flag that the Fire Department had raised on the ladder truck; it was high above and waving gently in the breeze. Suddenly, about half a block from the church, a black sedan whipped out of a side street; the three dudes in it pitched bags of fast food garbage and big gulps at us from the window. Though they missed us and just sped away, we all just stood there speechless, shaking our heads. It was a surreal experience for sure, and it was the first time I realized how unpopular the war had become in this country.

Soon after, I was selected to serve as one of the founding operational members of the newly formed U.S. Marine Corps Special Operations Command (MARSOC), a command that would later be tasked with carrying on the legendary Marine Raider namesake.

I was assigned as a member of 2nd Marine Special Operations Battalion, Golf Company, Direct Action Special Reconnaissance Platoon, team Alpha; we deployed to Afghanistan in late summer 2007. About this same time, my best friend and teammate, Danny, and I became two of the first "poster boys" for Marine Special Operations when we were both featured on a MARSOC recruiting poster in early 2007. That poster would later hang in New York City, not far from the very building that Danny stood atop in 2001 while witnessing the twin towers fall. Danny is a true warrior and a great friend in every sense; and I have often referred to him as my "guardian angel" because we have survived so much together.

On September 25, 2007, during a routine combat reconnaissance patrol south of Musa Quala, our Marine Special Operations Team (MSOT) was surrounded and ambushed by hundreds of Taliban fighters in Afghanistan's Helmand Providence. A vicious battle ensued and six of us were wounded when one of our vehicles was struck with rounds from an 82mm recoilless rifle.

Our team's Special Operations Medic, and brother, Charles Luke Milam, would die on that hill moments later, as we continued to fight and save the rest of the wounded with the skills he had taught us. The explosion had cut Luke in half; I take some solace in the fact that he didn't suffer for long. Gary suffered two femoral bleeds from shrapnel and Joe had a giant piece of metal jammed deep in his calf. Marcus, Donkey, Drake and I all suffered from proximity blast concussions from the massive explosion.

The death of a close friend is one of the shittiest things I have ever had to witness.

I still remember the first thing that popped into my head as I looked over at Luke dying: "I'm glad that's not me," and then immediately felt incredibly guilty about having that thought. That intense guilt remained for years to come.

Then a sick feeling in the pit of my stomach settled in as I looked around at the bloody butchery inflicted on my team. I was terrified in that moment, yet I had to convince myself to do the right thing: continue to fight and help stop the bleeding of the wounded.

I found Danny and Pat and Will, and we went to work. The memories from that day would prove to be haunting, yet I also witnessed incredible courage and valor as my teammates rushed all over the battlefield. Running around exposed, dodging mortar, rocket and machine gun fire, repelling the enemy's onslaught and treating and evacuating our wounded teammates.

Days later, official reports said that our Special Operations Company had killed over 100 enemy fighters, in a battle that raged for nearly two days straight! The remainder of the deployment was filled with missions just as crazy and dangerous as they are made out to be in the movies; and we ended up killing around 300 enemy fighters in something like three months. It seemed like every time we left the base we would find a fight. It was the first time we had ever deployed to combat in a Special Operations unit, and we were literally baptized by fire! It was a gunfighter's dream: near-constant, vigorous and manic.

It seemed that everyone from that deployment ended up getting divorced shortly after returning from Afghanistan in early 2008; and if they didn't get divorced, their relationships were certainly tested. My own marriage failed because I just became an even worse alcoholic than I already was. That mixed with an increased operations tempo at work proved to be too much for Jennifer, and I don't blame her for leaving. When my wife left, she took almost everything and left me in an incredible amount of debt. Only a few short months later, she had a meltdown, and lost her job as a teacher. On my own now with no supervision, I began drinking until blackout every night.

In February 2009, I returned to Afghanistan with MSOT 8211. We were sent to Herat province in the western part of the country and began work trying to locate, hunt down and eliminate all Taliban activity in the area. 8211 was a team full of 20 or so very rough, battle-hardened Marine commandos who were more than hungry for a gunfight. Everyone on our team had previous combat experience either in Iraq or southern Afghanistan or both. We were the Fox Company's designated high altitude parachute team and more than half of us had been part of MARSOC since its inception three years prior.

There was a tremendous amount of experience on that team and it didn't hurt that our team chief was a legendary Force Recon Marine by name of Eden Pearl. Eden was a giant Viking of a man, whose battlefield reputation preceded him. He had worked for Doug Zembiec in Kosovo years earlier; we spoke of Doug affectionately and often. Eden helped develop the art of modern gunfighting within the Marine Special Operations schoolhouse, and today has the Marksmanship Award named after him. Watching Eden gunfight was like watching Bruce Lee do Kung Fu. Shooting alongside him was the first time in my professional career that I started to look at gunfighting as its own martial art; and this man was most certainly a master at it. His weapons manipulation and foot movement seemed fluid; his accuracy was surgical. We all learned a great deal from him and it would prove to serve us well in battle.

On August 1, 2009, during a vehicle patrol into a nearby village and suspected enemy safe haven, our team was ambushed from elevated positions and attacked from all directions. The enemy initiated the attack with a rocket-propelled grenade (RPG) that literally missed the truck that I was riding in by inches, and detonated into the wall behind us. The explosion was so close, I felt the shockwave pass through my body and I could literally taste the gasses from the explosion. Miraculously none of us were wounded; and our trucks machine gunner Big Tom swung the massive 50 caliber around like a water pistol and cut the second story off of a building from where the rocket was fired. Then all hell opened up on us from fighting positions located on both sides of the road with machine guns and more rockets.

As we began our counterattack and tried to navigate this ambush, one of our machine gunners, Garth, took an AK-47 round to the upper thigh that went through his femur, and he was losing a great deal of blood. I ran back through the ambush to help, with a Taliban sniper chasing me the entire way back down the street. Rounds smacked the wall inches from my head as I crouched and sprinted, screaming curses.

When I got to Garth, he looked gray and seemed to be fading in and out of consciousness. Our teammate, John, was able to pull him out of the truck while under fire, and to some cover where he applied the tourniquet that saved Garth's life.

We were pinned down in a street and surrounded. Harrison, our team Captain, told us air support would take about 55 minutes to reach us. Now we were on our own, and our team's Special Operations Medic, Sanki Oak, was telling us that Garth needed to get to a surgeon fast... or he wasn't going to make it.

That was all we needed to hear; with RPGs slamming into the walls on either side of the street, we loaded Garth up onto a stretcher and ran him through the gunfire to my truck and fought our way to a nearby Spanish base with a hospital and a landing strip. When we got to the base, the guards wouldn't open the gate without authorization or something.

Garth was in bad shape; he'd lost nearly 2 liters of blood. And I was fed up with the inefficiency of coalition warfare. I told Mike, my armored Gun Mobility Vehicle (GMV) driver, to ram the gate down. He did, and we saved Garth's life.

At this, Eden laughed... but told me later that we couldn't do that any more.

About two weeks later, on August 16, 2009, we found ourselves in the worst gunfight of my life. It was strange because we actually knew we would be attacked, but we figured that is what we were there for. 8211 had just executed a daring nighttime raid on two Taliban safehouses located 5 kilometers deep inside an enemy village called Afghanistan.

Initially we met minimal enemy resistance; a small enemy fire team was attempting to track our movement as we crept around the narrow, shadowed footpaths. The state-of-the-art night vision goggles we wore afforded us significant advantage as they washed our view of the pitch-black village in an eerie green glow.

The enemy fire team ended up walking directly into our rear security element in a pitch-black alleyway. Eden, Lou, Dennis, and Jake stitched up the enemy team pretty good with some carbine fire, which effectively halted their pursuit. One of the enemies was so startled that he accidently shot himself in the foot. The enemy then started probing my team as we hurried to finish our tasks.

Upon egress from the target area, our team was ambushed again. There was a massive explosion and then all hell broke loose from both sides of the road again. Rockets and machine gun tracers lit up the inky black night, and the all-too-familiar roar of battle broke the silence. I assumed the massive explosion was an IED. I tried the radios but when I got no response, I jumped from the safety of my armored chariot, and Danny and I rushed back together to see what had happened.

We gathered teammates and Afghan policemen who were working with us, and set up a defensive perimeter around one of our trucks that had been blown 20 feet into the air by a massive IED buried in the road. The truck landed upside down and ignited into white-hot flames that danced 30 feet tall.

Everything was on fire; ammunition was going off everywhere, and since this was our mini-gun truck, there were 9,000 machine gun rounds cracking off everywhere like evil firecrackers burning the shit out of people.

I knew as soon as I got close to the truck that it was Eden's. He and three others had been severely wounded when they were thrown from the vehicle during the blast while two of our teammates were trapped and killed in the burning wreckage.

As I was looking around for guidance or ideas or trying to figure out what the next right thing to do was; Lou rushed into the flames and recovered two anti-tank rockets that were on fire and dangerously close to cooking off. He was our team's bomb tech and he knew that if those rockets had gone off in that street, we all would've been fucked. I don't even want to imagine what would have happened if those rocket motors had ignited that night.

I looked around in shock at the sight of my brothers mangled in the street as enemy bullets cracked overhead. I couldn't believe this had happened to my team again.

John, Marc, Jason and Eden were all in very bad shape; we loaded them up in our medevac vehicles; our company headquarters that had been supporting our mission helped medevac our badly injured comrades. Jason actually manned a machine gun on the ride out as his leg hung on by a thread. The rest of us remained behind fighting and recovering the bodies of our fallen teammates Nick Roush and Uncle Ahmed. I knew that our team required organization, leadership, and direction, and I did my best to provide what I could that night.

The radios still weren't working and I ended up having to sprint from person to person in order to communicate and coordinate anything. I must have collectively run over a mile back and forth and up and down the street that night. My team was spread thin and had good dispersion locking down the street. But each time I took off I thought about that sniper from two weeks earlier who chased me down the wall, and I just hoped he wasn't out there. My teammates fought like Spartans to keep the enemy at bay, and we continued with our priorities of work.

Harrison was keeping everything together by communicating with the task force through what seemed to be our only working radio. When he wasn't helping me sort out the situation on the ground, he was also working with Fitty, our teams Joint Terminal Air Controller (JTAC). They were calling in fire all around us from the aircraft above and there were explosions going off everywhere. The scent of burning flesh and gun smoke filled the street; it felt like I was on some post-apocalyptic movie set.

After using every fire extinguisher we had recovering Nick's body from the blast site, the enemy began reinforcing from the eastern part of the village. The supporting aircraft had just reported that they were observing a large enemy force heading our direction and more enemy movement along our escape route. Then the aircraft told us they were out of fuel and had to head back to Bagram air base. This was an AC-130 Spectre Gunship that had been effectively keeping us alive all night. They had been providing dangerously close supporting fire and killing lots of enemy from 10,000 feet above for us. I knew we wouldn't last very long in that village without them. We had yet to recover Uncle Ahmed's body. But after some fucked up debate I was told to take point and navigate us to safety.

I found Danny, then we loaded up the remainder of our team and started to move out. Within a few short minutes, our convoy of trucks was attacked again. The enemy had set up a five-kilometer long ambush along the road, and it became clear that we were going to have to fight our way out of that village.

It seemed like it took forever as we sped down the road with rockets and machine gun tracers flying at us from all directions. The enemy had so many fighting positions that it was as if everyone in the village had woken up and wanted to kill us. Eddie, our truck's machine gunner cleared a path for us with the .50 cal and we kept moving forward.

It seemed like as soon as we hit the paved road and made it out of that living nightmare, the sun began to rise in the east. An eerie silence came over everyone as we sped the 10 miles back to our base. No one spoke on the radio, and no one spoke inside our truck. The energy was very heavy as every one of us mentally processed what we had just survived. I felt like crying and shutting down. I was sick to my stomach and felt completely drained and I wanted to quit. But then I was reminded of something Doug Zembiec had told me once years prior: "Live for the mission;" and it reminded me that our mission was not over yet.

MSOT 8212 and a Special Forces team would recover Uncle Ahmed's body the following night. About a week later, an Army psychologist flew out to our base and spoke with each one of us individually. I had never spoken to a head doctor before, but I hadn't slept in five days, so I was willing to try anything at the time. She certainly helped our team heal a little bit and be functional again since we still had three months left on our nine-month deployment.

About that same time, Abe and I had the honor and privilege of speaking at the memorial service for my teammates Nick Roush and Ahmed; I feel like we honored them well. It was difficult, but helpful for me to convey the immense loss that our team was feeling at that time.

Our team had suffered two Killed in Action (KIA) and five severely Wounded in Action (WIA) within a two-week period. Jason lost his leg, Marc had to get rebuilt, Garth was all fucked up, John was in a coma for close to two months, and Eden was being called the most injured man to ever survive his wounds.

I tried to keep it together for the rest of that deployment because my teammates needed me to. It was difficult because I felt responsible for flaws in my planning that allowed everything to happen. I felt like I had failed. When I returned from that deployment, I entered a realm of alcoholism that I honestly believe most people never recover from. I drank myself to sleep every single night for the next three years straight.

My girlfriend, Amanda, and I had the most amazing baby girl in 2010. We named her Devyn, and she is absolutely fearless. I have definitely screwed up a lot of good things in my life, but I am so grateful that I never lost my little family. They have been there by my side through everything and they helped save my life when I was at my darkest.

Following my deployment with 8211, I was promoted to Gunnery Sergeant and I was able to take a job as an instructor at the Marine Special Operations School; the component that is responsible for assessing, selecting, and training future Marine Raiders. I was proud of the responsibility that comes with training Critical Skills Operators (CSO), and it seemed like the perfect place to spend a few years while Amanda and Devyn and I started our life together.

I figured that I had amassed a great deal of experience that I could share with students, and impart valuable teachings. But I quickly found out that it was to be the most frustrating and thankless job I have ever had in my entire life.

My drinking and associated craziness continued to spiral out of control. More and more of my friends kept dying and I kept on dealing with it poorly. Every medal that my 8211 teammates and I had been submitted for ended up being downgraded by Headquarters Marine Corps (HQMC) with no explanation.

This was nothing new, of course, but strangely, we were the only team in the company that this was happening to, and our team leader, Harrison, personally apologized to us. I personally never cared about medals; I was just there for the combat and the brotherhood. But it was obviously affecting some of my teammates, so I tried to figure it out. I was never given a clear answer. It is my opinion that many heroes had been robbed of recognition.

Every instructor in my section was overworked and underappreciated. My self-worth was in the shitter. By mid-2012, I was drinking every night and had a negative outlook on everything. It was a strange time in my life, as I was very close to rock-bottom, and I knew it, but I didn't know what to do about it. I spent a lot of nights cross-eyed drunk and staring at a shotgun next to my bed... and a few nights with it in my mouth. More and more of my friends kept dying, and I felt this incredible guilt for being alive.

Things at work just continued to get worse. I was getting increasingly angry and felt extremely isolated. I don't know if others around me were able to notice, but I left work feeling close to unglued. I recognized then that I most likely required the help of a medical doctor, but I honestly didn't even know where to start.

I can honestly say that is the point where I lost all trust in anyone and became extremely defensive to everyone I encountered.

And I went to the bottle. A week or two later, I went on an incredible bender, drinking whiskey by the bottle, blowing money and partying for the next two days straight. It ended up being the last time I ever drank.

That September, I got myself blackout drunk and experienced what doctors would help me later recognize as a flashback, the combination of which had dire consequences. I mindlessly committed a heinous act without any awareness or conscious thought at the time, and soon after realized that I'd finally hit rock bottom. I felt like my life was over, like I would never be able to recover from this. I committed myself to the idea of suicide. A friend of mine intervened and brought me to a mental hospital where I would spend the next two weeks.

I was heavily medicated for those first two weeks and I honestly don't remember much. I was dealing with alcohol withdrawals, physical and emotional, as well as facing all of my life's madness head-on sober for the first time in my life. It was intense! I felt safe, being surrounded by medical professionals, but I didn't trust anyone in my early recovery, and I still planned to kill myself or vanish as soon as I got the opportunity.

Telling my story made me wonder if I should be proud of myself or ashamed of myself for not having committed suicide yet. I hated the pity that people gave me. It wasn't until I was transferred to the Camp Lejeune Naval Hospital psychiatric unit that I stopped having those incredibly dark thoughts.

That happened one day, when I met a woman named Ann Marie, who taught a yoga class at the hospital. She was one of the first people that I trusted in my early recovery; I couldn't even trust my doctor in that facility. But Ann Marie had such an amazing energy that it somehow broke down that wall for me. She was a natural healer and I honestly believe she helped save my life with a single yoga class. We have been great friends ever since.

She broke me from my comfort zone of self-containment and I walked out of that class surprisingly optimistic for the first time in the better part of a decade.

I had never done yoga before, and I couldn't believe how centered and refreshed I felt immediately afterward. I smiled for the first time in months and I slept like a baby that night. Life came into focus for me over the next few days and I felt like a different person. I realized that I was facing some of the biggest challenges of my entire life — I am a person who looks for challenges — and Recovery became my mission.

I later had to go to court with my attorney and a letter from the MARSOC Commanding General, requesting to attend a dual-diagnosis PTSD and substance abuse program instead of weekly AA meetings.

My situation was not a secret, and I encountered detractors at every turn. I was ostracized at work and very few people even spoke to me.

At first it was hard to not feel abandoned and betrayed. But after a while I didn't focus on it; I had a mission again: recovering and helping others to recover.

I had no real example to follow. I didn't know anyone who had ever been in the same situation as me, but I was committed to figuring it out myself. I talked and shared my story with anyone who would listen; and I was even able to travel to SOCOM HQ in Tampa to speak with members of the Special Operations Forces Care Coalition (SOFCC) as well as the Command Sergeant Major.

In August 2013, after much posturing between my military attorney and the MARSOC Commanding General, I was administratively separated from the Marine Corps. I went before a judge on October 14, 2013. I had a pretty incredible attorney who looked like something straight out of The Devil's Advocate, and we had been preparing for the worst-case scenario since day one. I had a lot of support from my family and teammates but it was still the stressful equivalent of walking into a gunfight. However, I had been in far worse situations with worse odds.

I was fortunate that the judge took my military service into account: 14 years of active-duty service, a veteran of two wars, 20 medals, including the Purple Heart and two medals for heroic achievement on the battlefield, hundreds of combat missions in support of the Global War on Terrorism, featured on two special operations recruiting posters, Recon Sniper, one of the first Marine Raiders since World War II and 73 very powerful character witness statements from friends and teammates. My attorney also told the court about my mission and what I had been able to accomplish in the year leading up to then.

I returned to Connecticut. I had just lost my career and I was completely broke with no plan. I was 80% disabled; and I didn't even have an honorable discharge.

With no resources to attempt a discharge upgrade, finding any type of gainful employment has been pretty much impossible. But I haven't lost faith, I am confident that someday someone will give me an opportunity and I won't let it go to waste.

For now, I continue to focus on my mission and my family. In the past couple years, I have been able to inspire and encourage others to seek treatment for PTSD and a few people have even told me that I helped save them in that respect. One night I was even able to help stop the suicide of a fellow Marine.

I'm proud to say that it has been over three years now since my last drink, and I honestly don't miss it one bit.

I do not consider myself recovered from PTSD by any means, but remaining sober has been the most important aspect of my recovery.

More of my friends have died, and I still have terrible days, but the terrible days no longer come every day. Nowadays I wake up looking forward to everything that life has to offer.

I am honestly grateful and a little impressed that I am still alive and roaming this planet. I am learning more and more as my mission progresses and I feel like I am headed in the right direction.

Along my journey, I have learned that there are all different types of warriors fighting all different types of battles. I continue to search for opportunities to help others, no matter who they are now, and consequently, the more people I help, the more "recovered" I feel.

I imagine that I will continue on this mission for a long time; it has become a healing journey for me and it has been incredible.

I am certainly embarrassed and ashamed of the mistakes I have made along the way, but I don't regret a thing that has happened. How could I? I am now a better man because of it all, and because of this, others have emerged better people as well. I have grown so much in such a short period of time, and I owe it all to my family and the amazing friends that I have made along the way. I am proud of the things that my friends and I have accomplished and I will always remember my brothers who died the warrior's death. We lived our dream, and it was awesome!

I don't know if what I am doing now will ever completely fix me, but I do know that I have helped change lives for the better. If I keep going, then there just might be some hope. ✧

GySgt Adam Kinosh enlisted in the U.S. Marine Corps on July 19, 1999. He graduated October 15, 1999. From November 1999 to December 1999, he attended the School of Infantry at Camp Geiger, North Carolina to become a Marine Rifleman. From December 1999 to September 2001, he was assigned as a rifleman to Second Marine Division, 2nd Light Armored Reconnaissance Battalion, where he completed NBC Monitor, Survey Course, and Scout Swimmers Course, and was promoted to the rank of LCpl.

He served one unit deployment with the 22nd MEU (SOC) from September 2001 to July 2006. He was assigned to 2nd Marine Division, 2nd Reconnaissance Battalion, where he served as a Reconnaissance Scout, Assistant Team Leader, Reconnaissance Training Platoon Instructor, and eventually as a Team Leader where he achieved the rank of Sergeant. He completed Basic Reconnaissance Course, Airborne School, HRST Master, Scout Sniper School, Urban Sniper Course, Advanced Reconnaissance and Surveillance Course, SERE Level "C," Marine Combat Instructor of Water Survival. He completed a combat deployment to Iraq in 2005-2006, and was awarded the Navy Achievement Medal and Combat Action Ribbon.

In July 2006, GySgt Kinosh was hand-selected to serve as one of the founding members of the Marine Corps Forces Special Operations Command (MARSOC; he would become one of the first Marine Raiders since World War II). From July 2006 to February 2008, he was assigned to Marine Corps Forces Special Operations Command, 2nd Marine Special Operations Battalion, Company "G," where he achieved the rank of SSgt. While in Golf Company, GySgt. Kinosh completed the Merlin Close Target Surveillance Course, in Hereford, England, the MARSOC Advanced Sniper Course, and the Dynamic Assault/Special Reconnaissance Course. He served one combat deployment with Golf Company to Afghanistan in 2007-2008, where he was awarded the Purple Heart, the Navy and Marine Corps Commendation Medal with combat distinguishing device and Combat Action Ribbon.

From March 2008 to January 2010, GySgt Kinosh was assigned to Marine Corps Forces, Special Operations Command, 2d Marine Special Operations Battalion, Fox Company, Marine Special Operations Team 1, Element Leader, and eventually serving as Operations SNCO and interim Team Chief. He completed one combat deployment with Fox Company to Afghanistan and received a second Navy Commendation Medal with combat distinguishing device. From January 2010 until February 2011, GySgt Kinosh was assigned to Marine Corps Forces, Special Operations Command, 2d Marine Special Operations Battalion, H&S co S-3 TCell.

From February 2011 until 2013 GySgt Kinosh was assigned to the Marine Special Operations School, Serving as the Lead Amphibious Operations Instructor, Chief Instructor and section SNCOIC. While serving there, GySgt Kinosh completed the Formal Schools Instructor Course, Senior Instructors Course and the EWTGPAC Maritime Navigation Course. ✦

Michael Le Buhn

Someday you'll be alone,
Way out there in that Combat Zone.
Bullets flyin all around
Keep your head low to the ground.
Don't you worry about being alone,
Alpha Outlaws gonna bring you home.

Here's how I remember it:

As a child, I did not have to wonder what I would be when I grew up. My future was already written; or so it seemed. My father was, and still is, perhaps the greatest pastor I have ever been around. My grandmother was a pastor, as were both of my uncles and most of my adult cousins. We are a family of pastors. I suppose if I had been born to a family of doctors or politicians, I would have accepted my fate just as readily. I was more than resigned to my lot in life, however; I was excited! I wanted to be a minister. I looked up to my dad like any young boy and I was convinced that being a pastor was the most significant job in the world. Recipients of a good pastor's leadership and guidance wouldn't hesitate to support such an endorsement. It seemed only natural, when I began preaching at 15 years old. I was well on my way to becoming a young successful minister when I received my ministerial license at 18 years old and my first full-time job on a pastoral team at 19. I was thrilled. At this rate, I would be a senior pastor by the time I was 25, and life would be daisies.

There was one problem hiding in the dark corners of my mind, however. From time to time, I would be forced to confront this problem, as it would occasionally spring up between thoughts. I would be in a conversation with a Christian friend or colleague regarding the theological underpinnings of some ludicrous doctrine belonging to a rival religious ideology, and out of nowhere, I would catch myself thinking something like, "Michael, the only reason you believe differently than the people you are criticizing is because of the family you were born to, the country and year you were born in, or the different experiences you've had comparatively, which simply amount to bad or dumb luck." Thoughts like that are dangerous.

Suddenly, I was slow to subscribe to even the most casual commitment to the sort of theological or metaphysical superiority my church boasted as a means to strengthen cohesion within the group; a chorus which I'd joined all-too-readily just weeks before. I couldn't shake it, though. Every time I would start to make some claim regarding the absolute superiority of my religion over another, I was immediately confronted with the fact that the only thing separating me, then a Pentecostal minister and a minister's son, from a Muslim, was the conditions surrounding my birth. Had I been born in Baghdad instead of Little Rock and to Muslim parents instead of Christian, there is no reason to believe I would have believed any less zealously in Islam than I did in Christianity at the time.

Why should I think my resolve would have been any different if my parents had raised me to pray to a god by a different name than the God I inherited? This shook my belief structure to the core. Suddenly the difference between eternal life and death did not seem like the difference between good and evil, but rather the difference of heads or tails on an unfair coin toss.

Was I to believe that I was born again, saved, sanctified, and filled with the Holy Ghost, (and on my way to Heaven, "Say, 'Amen!'") by the mere chance of my Christian birth? Or was there some darker, more morbid answer? Was God to blame? Did He know before I was born (as the book of Jeremiah seems to insinuate) that I would live as a Christian and go to Heaven? Did He choose for me to be fortunate enough to be born into the right religion while the rest of the world was just shit outta luck? Well, how did I get so lucky? Why would He let so many be born into false religions if all of the well-intentioned members of these false religions are just gonna be turned around at the Pearly Gates anyway? ("Say, 'Amen?'")

I had believed in God since before my first memories, and even in this serious crisis, I still didn't question the existence of God. That came later. I was certainly beginning to lose my faith in the church, though. I wasn't sure it was accomplishing its mission, and, more immediately, I was beginning to feel certain that I did not have a place in that world. I couldn't continue to represent an institution that, in my opinion, ostracized so many people; it became obvious that I needed to find another path.

I researched career paths and spent a tremendous amount of time in thought and prayer, when, one day, it all became so clear for me. I was sitting in a Taco Bell admiring a WWII Veteran's hat which showed his former unit's insignia, pins for this and that, etc. It reminded me of my grandfather's hat, which was so similar. I couldn't help but associate my grandfather's military service with my concept of who he was. The same was true of my father! My dad was a Navy man when he and my mother fell in love through love letters while Dad was in Sicily, and Mom was in Marshall, Arkansas… Mars and Venus, respectively. Military Service Members and Veterans were living heroes to me, and my father and grandfather stood in their ranks! I thanked the Taco Bell Veteran for his service and listened as he told amazing stories from his time in the service. I had been considering a military career, but as I looked at that old veteran, I was overwhelmed by one thought that I immediately blurted out to my wife, Casey; "Casey, I don't want to end up an old man with no hat."

A few months later, I pretended I wasn't scared to death as I waved farewell to my wife, mother, and father, and left for Basic Training. Basic Training, like most things in life, was not nearly as bad as the fear of Basic Training. In no time flat, the same Drill Sergeants who, just 9 weeks earlier had evoked terror in me, shook my hand and called me "Soldier," (a huge improvement on "jack-baller," which was their favorite insult throughout my BCT Company. When pushed to answer the question, "Drill Sergeant, what exactly is a 'jack-baller?' every Drill Sergeants answer was the same; "YOU ARE A JACK-BALLER, JACK-BALLER!"), causing me to wonder why I had ever been afraid to begin with.

I reported to Ft. Hood in February of 2006 and my Command Sergeant Major told me in our first meeting, "Don't even let your wife unpack, son. You're going to war." I'll never forget that drive home, knowing I had to break the news to Casey that my choice to join the Army was going to hold more immediate and permanent consequences than either of us were ready to face.

I was luckier than I knew, though. As luck would have it, I landed in the single best unit that the United States Army had to offer: Outlaws! The group of men and women that I went to war with were the cream of the crop. They were committed, fearless leaders all the way down, and early on, I knew that I was lucky to count myself among them. We were already waist-deep in pre-deployment preparations when I arrived, and those months at Ft. Hood leading up to our deployment to Iraq in October 2006 remain a blur. I remember Iraq like it was yesterday, though. Those memories will never be far away.

We arrived in Baghdad and our company split into approximately 10 different teams to be dispersed throughout all of Iraq. I remember clearly my first night in Iraq. I was assigned to a team of four soldiers who would be stationed at Convoy Support Command Scania (Skan-yuh). We were scheduled to fly via Blackhawk the next morning from Baghdad International Airport (BIAP) to

Scania and only had about 5 hours of shut-eye before we had to prep and leave. The other members of our team fell asleep long before me, and I remember lying in my bunk wondering how I ever got so far from home. I remember wishing I had a child who would carry on my bloodline in case I didn't live through the deployment. The last thing I remember thinking before drifting off to wherever it is we go when we sleep, was how selfish of me it was to wish a child existed, only to suffer from the loss of his or her father if I died. Perhaps I wouldn't reproduce, but if I was going to die, it seemed I should feel relieved that there wouldn't be a fatherless child left to suffer from my death. I had always wanted a child, but it was selfish to even dream of having a child only to check out and leave an already grieving widow with a child to care for alone… oh, the things soldiers will tell themselves just to fall asleep.

On the flight into Scania, the other three members of my team; SGT Gonzalez, SGT Scott, and SSG Porter (all of which outranked me) piled into one Blackhawk and I had to ride in the tailing Blackhawk with the gear. As luck would have it, my Blackhawk took small arms fire. Small arms fire is no serious threat to a Blackhawk. Nevertheless, it did feel like a very fitting "Welcome to Iraq!"

That warm sentiment was echoed later that night when I experienced my first mortar attack. I hadn't been in country for even 48 hours and I was already sitting in a bunker cracking jokes with strangers and wondering how long it would be until I could smoke a cigarette. This was a scene I would grow incredibly accustomed to.

Christmas came and went and before I knew it. 2007 had arrived as my friend and I brought in the New Year with the closest thing to champagne we could find: Nyquil cut with Red Bull. Unfortunately, 2007 proved to be about as good a year as Red Bull/Nyquil was champagne. We were getting bombed almost nightly. It became so common for us to come under attack that when a night would go by without an attack I would find myself feeling agitated and nervous, waiting for the other shoe to drop. And drop it did.

In February of 2007, on the very day I decided to quit smoking cigarettes, we suffered a devastating attack. The enemy had someone inside our camp who had drawn a map of our base, allowing them to strategically bomb our dining facility, our gym, our chapel, and our living quarters, all within just a few minutes. As our retaliatory forces advanced on them, crossing a bridge about 1 kilometer from our base, the bridge exploded with multiple IEDs. The damage to our soldiers and equipment was devastating, and when our quick-reaction force tried to provide reinforcements, they were ambushed as well. In short, we got our asses kicked.

I was standing in my room when the blast from the explosion threw me against the wall. I yelled, "INCOMING!" but could not hear the words coming from my mouth as I was temporarily deaf as a result of the explosion. It didn't matter, I didn't know it at the time, but I was alone in our living quarters. (*Someday you'll be alone*) I remember running to the bunker with my rifle, vest and Kevlar in tow. As I put on my gear in the bunker, I tried to remember what I was supposed to do (*Way out there in that Combat Zone*). I still couldn't hear anything, but every few seconds, my hands would involuntarily jump to my ears as my body was reacting to the subsequent explosions even though I couldn't consciously hear them going off around me (*Bullets flyin' all around*).

Then, as though someone was holding the 'volume up' button on the world, my hearing returned in a wave in my uninjured ear. What I heard was unforgettable. I heard men screaming. Until that moment, I had never heard men scream in terror. In the midst of so much chaos, completely cloaked in darkness, not knowing if we were being overrun or not, I heard a chorus of men screaming in agony, in fear, and in confusion. Some were leaders who couldn't find the soldiers under their command. Some were wounded and suffering. Many more were with the wounded, dead, or dying and they screamed for help. I heard voices I recognized. Men who were the picture of strength and courage were now, in the middle of an attack, trying desperately to reestablish control of the situation and gain accountability for their teams.

I was alone.

We started as a team of four, but SGT Gonzalez had been reassigned to Forward Operating Base Kalsu, leaving just the three of us, and the other two were across the base at our office. I was under strict orders to wait in the nearest bunker until discovered by one of my two Non Commissioned Officers (NCO's). I waited, as ordered, but I didn't have to wait long. Still, in those moments alone, I experienced fear like I had never experienced it before in my life. I was no more convinced that I would survive the night than I was convinced I would die. I remember closing my eyes. I took off my sock and shoved it into the ear that was bleeding and put my Kevlar on so no one would know I was hurt. I asked God to help me know what to do, to give me courage, to help me not let my friends down in this life-or-death situation (*Keep your head low to the ground*).

Miraculously, I felt completely relieved of my fear (*Don't you worry about being alone*). I felt steel replace my spine and I started checking my gear for any and all first aid equipment. Just then, SSG Porter and SGT Scott appeared in my bunker having run across the base with mortars and rockets landing around them just to get to me (*Alpha Outlaws gonna bring you home*).

"SSG Porter, you got a cigarette?" I asked as he walked into the bunker.

"I got you covered, Le Buhn," as he handed me a Newport and filled me in on what was going on and how we were going to proceed.

Over the years, I've reflected on that night and tried to make sense of everything that happened. At the time, it didn't feel like it was going to be one of the most significant days of my life. I felt an array of emotions and was eventually just happy I got through it. But through my efforts to understand that night, somehow consistent with the rest of my life (at the unrelenting demands of my VA therapist!), I have realized something paramount about my personal faith. Although I was disenfranchised by the exclusivity, or perceived exclusivity of the message my church subscribed to, I never doubted the message itself; I just want it to extend to everyone. And although I have, off and on throughout the years, doubted the plausibility of an all-powerful, all-knowing, creator of the Universe, "God," I have never stopped believing in Him.

Faith is a funny thing. It seems to me that if someone has faith in something, then they necessarily do not have proof of it. My belief in God relies on my faith. Should I possess any irrefutable proof of His existence then my faith would no longer exist. I may not have the will or desire to be a spokesperson for a faith that makes claims to a more perfect interpretation or understanding of God, but I cannot deny the fact that on that night in Iraq I was afraid, I asked for courage from God and my fear disappeared and I felt safe and strong. This is certainly not scientific proof of the existence of God, but it serves as a renewable source of fuel to the fire of my faith in a God that hears even insignificant me when I ask for help.

I later received a Purple Heart for my injury, though I hardly felt worthy. I told SGT Scott later that I didn't feel right wearing it and had decided not to include it on my Class A Uniform unless I was specifically directed to do so for a military board appearance or something. SGT Scott understood that I felt unworthy because so many people were injured more severely than I that night. A friend of ours had lost his life that night.

"Wear it for him then," he told me; "If you don't feel worthy enough to wear it for you, wear that Purple Heart for our fallen friend since he can't wear his anymore."

I've worn my Purple Heart proudly for those heroes ever since. Perhaps my injuries didn't merit award in my eyes, but their sacrifice was absolute. They deserve only the highest honor. So on the advice of my squad leader, SGT Scott, I puffed my chest out and displayed that medal proudly for them; for all of them that sacrificed and died in the name of this country.

Once I came home from Iraq, I had every intention of leaving the military in pursuit of a more quiet life and career. Ha! Shortly after returning from war, my buddy invited me to attend a recruitment brief at Ft. Hood. I declined, as I could not imagine an offer the Army could make that would make me consider staying in the military. He then told me that if I attended the brief I would get out of work three hours early and I quickly made plans to attend the brief! The recruiters had come from the White House Communications Agency and I thought there was no way in Hell they would ever take a guy like me.

But, despite all my doubts, in February of 2009, I reported to the White House Communications Agency having re-enlisted for four more years. How could I turn it down? It was a once-in-a-lifetime opportunity, and I was so excited to start this new chapter in my life.

Things are rarely as they seem, however, and the excitement of the location of my job was quickly extinguished by the reality of my work. I was working in the accounting section of the agency and most of my day consisted of meetings and numbers, calculator, spreadsheets, computers and a growing disdain for my existence! Luckily, I had the honor of serving with some of the best leaders that the military has to offer and they quickly picked up on my boredom and waning morale. They decided to train me with the agency's audio/visual crew, and in no time, I was traveling around the globe with the President and Vice President of the United States. My job dealt with soundboards and microphones, new towns and strange cities, with a few stamps in my passport to boot. I loved my job!

On August 6, 2010, my daughter P was born. She was about a month early and was the single smallest baby I had ever seen in my life. All my life, I wanted to be a father. I wonder what kind of adult she will grow up to be if I don't feed her any of the normal bullshit that most kids hear on a daily basis. From the day she was born, I never talked to her like a baby. I certainly showed excitement in my voice, but I try to always remember that she isn't "just a kid," she is already a person. And furthermore, genetically, she is more closely related to me than anyone else on the planet, save my mother and father. With this in mind, I try to anticipate what she will think and what she will need and then provide it for her before the need is even fully realized. In short, I spoil the shit out of her.

Sometime in 2011, I sat her down and had a long talk with her, but she refused to quit growing while I was away on work. I explained that I was working for the President of the United States, and it was a once-in-a-lifetime opportunity, and all I really needed was for her to schedule her major milestones and growth spurts around my days off, but she only blew spit bubbles at me and then farted (admittedly, my methods were not very effective when she was an infant). So in December of 2012, having just come through an intense re-election season, I said farewell to the White House Communications Agency and set my sights on home and fatherhood.

Once again, however, things were not exactly as they seemed. When I returned home from war in December of 2007, having spent 15 long months in Iraq, I hardly resembled the man who raised his right hand and swore to protect his country. I had been a minister; a preacher. My entire existence revolved around human interaction and relationships. Once I returned home from war, I could hardly complete a task as simple as grocery shopping, since every time I entered a grocery store, I was constantly looking behind me. I felt an overwhelming sense of anger when people would block me in an aisle with their shopping carts to stare dumbly at the artichoke hearts. I didn't know why I was angry, I just was.

It was months before I was even able to sleep in the comfort of my bed (usually opting for the couch, a problem I still struggle with), and suddenly, other people's emotions were overwhelming for me. There was a time when I was really useful in situations where people were very upset, having recently lost a loved one, experienced some personal tragedy, or a failed relationship. Hell, as a minister that is the name of the game! Once I came home from Iraq, however, other people's negative emotions felt like insurmountable forces all collapsing on my position. My wife, parents, or even a co-worker would begin to cry for some arbitrary reason, and I would simply walk away thanking God I'd escaped.

Anger was always just below the surface for me, though. It was easily accessible to me in any situation, warranted or not. Even more troubling, for a long time it was the only emotion that was accessible to me at all. Before the birth of my daughter, I found it nearly impossible to feel love for anyone, and it was completely impossible for me to feel loved by anyone. It's hard to explain why I felt this way. Much of my feelings about war revolved around wishing I'd been able to do more. Many soldiers had a much more difficult tour than I. Many soldiers had much harder jobs where their lives were in greater danger more often than mine. During the months I was in Iraq, soldiers were far more likely to be killed by improvised explosive devices, mortars, or rockets than small arms fire, but that didn't change the fact that many soldiers stationed alongside me had fewer comforts than I. Many soldiers who wore the same Purple Heart that I wore had lost limbs, been disfigured, or narrowly escaped with their lives. How could I be counted among them?

Drinking helped. Well, drinking pretended to help. I could laugh when I drank. I could sleep when I drank. So, I always drank. I used to gleefully announce "I know what happens when I drink, I have no idea what happens when I don't so… Here's to the devil I know!" as I would throw back a swallow of bourbon (I enjoyed gin, scotch, most whiskeys and every kind of beer, but bourbon was my favorite). I didn't think my drinking was a problem because I was always in control in my own mind. I based this on the fact that I could go months without drinking when I put my mind to it, and felt no physical withdrawal symptoms. Perhaps that was the trickiest symptom of my Post Traumatic Stress Disorder; the illusion of control. I always thought I was deciding to drink, deciding to get drunk, and deciding to stay that way. An inebriated state of consciousness just seemed preferable when I wasn't working, so that is what I chose to do. It wasn't until much later that I realized just how much my drinking was motivated by PTSD. I had been a very responsible drinker before the war and once I returned I drank like a fish. But why? What was I running from? What was I hiding from? What exactly was I trying to medicate with all this medicine? And why was this happening to me when my tour was no worse than so many soldiers who returned home just fine? I wasn't even close to capable of even addressing these kinds of questions properly until I left the Army.

Unfortunately for me, the way my symptoms presented themselves made them almost undetectable while working for the White House. I drank, but almost exclusively after work. Most nights I would go straight to the bar after work, and then I'd fall asleep with a glass of bourbon in my hand in front of the television, but I was up and ready for work the next morning.

The reason I was drinking was to calm my nerves. I was always nervous, no matter where I was or who I was around. This made me very good at certain aspects of my job. Never feeling safe is to never let one's guard down, and I was an expert at that. Operational Security was my watchword and my paranoia was easily mistaken as attention to detail. I found myself uncomfortable in most situations, though when I feel uncomfortable I usually crack jokes. This was well received in the military as there is a long tradition of "class clown" types in the ranks. My missions typically went off without a hitch because I was constantly trying to ascertain what threats there could be to our mission success and then I would work to mitigate the chances of that happening. My hyper-vigilance and social anxiety made me easy to work with in such a rare professional environment and I was saved, more than once, by my innate ability to perform well under pressure. But when I left the White House with dreams of a normal life, I realized that, for me, a typical life would be a harder undertaking than the atypical one I walked away from.

As I mentioned, it was impossible for me to feel loved by anyone, even my family. My parents, my sister, and my wife did their best to communicate that they loved me but I knew deep down inside that they were talking to the Michael who had never gone to war. The Michael who knew how to laugh sober. The Michael who cared deeply, about everything. I was not that man. I was hard, angry, and cynical. I knew how ugly the world could be. I had seen the effects of the weapons we had made to destroy one another and I had lived in a country where everyone wanted me dead. In my mind, I wasn't the person my family loved; they still hadn't met me. They loved the boy who left for war. They didn't know the man who had returned.

I learned how to isolate myself from the people in my life internally. I figured out how to compartmentalize my life in such a way that I could be alone and safe, no matter who I was with. The numb feeling I once drank to avoid became the very goal of my drinking until my daughter complicated things. For one, I could no longer pretend to be devoid of emotion. One look at my little girl and I was in love and everybody knew it ("He IS capable of it! The jig is up!"). Perhaps it was because she was new. She was born long after I got back from Iraq and I was comforted knowing that she knew only me; she had no history with the pre-war Michael everyone else missed so much. She never knew me to be a minister or a patient man, she only knew me and that was fine. I decided that if I could do one thing right, I would be a good dad.

This didn't seem too difficult a task as I had an excellent example in my own father. My dad, ever the pastor, had devoted his life to the Church. He was and still is a man of the utmost integrity. I would put the purity my father's intentions against anyone in history and the best anyone else could hope for would be a draw. He wasn't perfect, no one is. But no one ever tried harder to be a good man than my dad. I felt obligated to do at least that for my daughter. So I decided I could not ever let her see me drunk. This meant longer periods of sobriety and those times of sobriety were always filled with joy. This joy, this love for my daughter, spread like an aggressive fucking cancer throughout my life.

Finally, it became clear that I had to get help. I was coming to terms with the bad choice that I had made over and over to hide my nightmares and feelings of worthlessness, feelings of shame, feelings of hate or numbness; I was tired of hiding all of it under gallons of bourbon when they just kept floating up to the top anyway. What was worse than the bad choice to defensively drink was the bad choices I would make when I was drunk. People were suffering simply because they were involved in my life and this had to stop. A few too many people hurt by my shit life, and a few too many shots of bourbon, and I was staring into the void contemplating the end of my existence. I had been chasing a feeling, any feeling. I had been chasing the eradication of all feelings. I had been looking for love and running from it. I had longed for sleep but evaded dreams, and I couldn't do it anymore. I thought long and hard about suicide. I considered it from every angle. I believed that the people in my life would be better off; well, most of them. But what about my daughter?

So I did some research. Turns out, killing yourself is by far the worst thing you can do as a parent. Who knew!? It was clear that if I wanted to be a good dad there was no way out. I had to just start being better. I realized that with no way out, I had to adapt to my new existence and overcome my new obstacles. In doing so, I survived the second threat of war; veteran suicide. Every single day, 22 veterans commit suicide (and this number doesn't include all 50 states as some don't report veteran suicides to the VA). War has claimed so many more lives than the ones lost in battle that, in fact, we lose more veterans to suicide in a single calendar year than all the American lives lost in combat in the entire Iraq war combined. It is a phenomenon of epidemic proportions, and I am lucky it didn't claim my life. Still, I had to get a handle on all of this and forge a way ahead. I had to learn how to make a successful life out of the mess I had become.

Casey and I were dead broke once I stopped receiving a check from the military. I wasn't yet rated as disabled through the VA, and I started attending

Kankakee Community College so that I could receive the Post 9/11 GI Bill as a way to make ends meet. I was very attracted to Psychology as it was helping me understand my existence. Naturally I was drawn to Philosophy as well since it asks a broader question, "What does it mean to exist?" These pursuits, along with the invaluable relationships I made through higher learning, have served as the background and setting for my road to a successful life while living with PTSD.

Now, I am starting my final semester as a senior at the University of Illinois with a double major in Psychology and Philosophy. This time next year I will be a college graduate and on my way to building whatever comes next. None of this would have been possible without my loved ones. They were so patient with me. They were so loving. So forgiving. And in a lot of ways, it was their love, the same love I couldn't feel when I came home, the same love I didn't believe in, along with the undeniable love for my daughter that pushed me to get the help I needed. I went to the VA and asked for help and they started me down the path that has led me to where I am now. I still suffer from PTSD. But now I have tools to deal with my symptoms. I don't try to drown them any longer and I am finally ok with who I am post-war and post-military.

I felt ruined for a long time. I was a Pentecostal hotshot! I was supposed to be a huge success personally, professionally, spiritually (if one can be 'spiritually successful.' I certainly used to think so), and now I can be found every year during Christmas shopping season leaning against the wall outside, smoking a cigarette, and trying to work up the courage to brave the line at Walmart (yes, I buy Christmas presents at Walmart. You should pity my loved ones for many reasons! Ha!). I started out as a preacher, and now the closest I come to preaching a sermon is when I do stand-up comedy twice a week. My how the mighty have fallen! Or have I?

When I look back on my life now, I don't feel like it shows a decline from moral fortitude to moral depravity. I don't compare my life to the life of the 20-year-old preacher I was when I joined the military. I don't ever wonder, even for a second, if I should be a preacher or a minister. It simply isn't for me. The way I see it, after 8 years in the military, 4 years at the White House, a Purple Heart, a Combat Action Badge, PTSD, five years a barfly, and some seriously burned bridges, I am no kind of candidate for the clergy; but I am a message. I'm not a preacher any more, but my life and the PTSD I deal with is a sermon to anyone willing to listen.

I don't resent my symptoms anymore. I don't hate them. I used to feel ashamed for struggling to reintegrate into society once I came back from war. I was embarrassed that I didn't recover from war like so many other soldiers could; soldiers who saw more suffering and suffered more than I. Some parts of me never left Iraq and I hated myself for that. I hated myself for not being able to muster up the twinkle in my eyes that existed before, I wanted so badly to be the innocent boy my parents remembered and looked for in me. But now I accept it. I'm okay with it. In fact, I gladly carry this heavy load.

I don't believe we, as human beings, should be capable of war. It is vicious. It is horrific. There is nothing more damaging to the human spirit than watching human beings needlessly suffer and die at the hands of other human beings, and in war, the suffering is too great to measure. Historically, we have measured the cost of war in lives lost. Our politicians decide who we should go to war with and then they send our forces out to battle in full confidence that we will kill more of them than they kill of us. And they are right. Our nation enjoys the most powerful military force in the history of the world. But even when we win in battle, we still lose something. For me, I lost my peace. I lost my belief in the beauty of the world for a long time. I was a human being who experienced an inhumane, inhuman environment and PTSD was the mark it left on me. And I am, in turn, the mark war left on America.

Just like the Purple Heart I wear as a symbol for, a message about, and a testament to the brave soldiers who were wounded and killed in battle; who can no longer wear their awards or stand in uniform, I carry Post Traumatic Stress Disorder as a symbol for, a message about, and a testament to the cost of winning a war. I am happy to be that message. I'm happy to have resigned as a preacher to become a sermon. And you can listen.

You can make it all worth something. You can hear this message every time you see one of us. We are relatively easy to spot. Our eyes are far too old for our age. Our tempers often hide the fact that even now we are fearing for our lives while we stand outside of shopping malls smoking cigarettes, or sit in restaurants with our backs always to the wall. We struggle with our personal relationships and often avoid talking about the war to people who have never been because, "they just won't understand." And they won't. But if you notice us, if you see the mark war left on our lives, if you can see us as the mark war left on our communities and our nation, then hear us. Hear the message our lives are screaming quietly from the cubicle next to you at work:

"War costs something. Even when we win. There is more than one way to lose a soldier. No one wins as long as there is war."

Life should be our watchword. Life should only be sacrificed to preserve more life. Our ultimate goal should not be global supremacy, political or ideological victory, nor should it be the hoarding of resources. Our nationalism should never be allowed to usurp the undeniable truth that life must be preserved and war should go extinct. I know it is impossible today, but perhaps it won't always be so. In the meantime, I'll keep pushing through if you promise to notice us. Remember us. Listen to the message of our lives. Things don't have to be this way forever. ✧

Michael Dennis Le Buhn Jr. is a comedian and was born in Little Rock, Arkansas in 1984. In September 2005, he joined the United States Army and in February 2006, he arrived at Ft. Hood, TX for his first duty assignment. In October of 2006, he deployed to Iraq with the First Calvary Division, where he was awarded the Purple Heart, a Combat Action Badge, and the Army Commendation Medal. After 15 months in Iraq, he redeployed to Ft. Hood, TX and was later recruited to work for the White House Communications Agency. From 2009 to 2013, he served in direct support of the President of the United States and was awarded the Presidential Service Badge, a Joint Service Achievement Medal and enjoyed the honor of winning Enlisted Person of the Year for the White House Communications Agency and the White House Military Office. He currently resides in Illinois with his wife and daughter and is a senior at the University of Illinois in Urbana/Champaign. ✦

jedimonk84@gmail.com

Nathaniel Lobas

As the saying goes, "the change is forever." These are the facts of my experience as a United States Marine as I remember them. All names have been altered so I don't get beat up or sued.

My name is Nathaniel Lobas. I am nearly 36 years old at this moment in time. I was born in 1979 near Cleveland, Ohio. My father was a firefighter. My mother cooked, cleaned, and took care of my brother and me. A working-class Catholic family.

After high school, I attended Ohio State University. I lived in a dorm room inside of the football stadium for a cut rate, which was supposed to be a privilege. There were no windows in the rooms, much like a bunker. I was unhappy, drinking and smoking too much. I disliked school, and felt like I was wasting my life there.

At OSU, I took a kayaking course to fulfill a recreation requirement. There were maybe 10 people in the kayaking class, which was designed to prepare us for our final exercise, a 10-day kayaking trip on the Rio Grande. My gear consisted of a dry bag, a sleeping bag, and a water bottle. I mostly ate refried beans out of the can.

I was fired up for the trip. We drove from Ohio to Texas in vans, found the river, and jumped into our kayaks. Most of the daytime was spent paddling, and we slept under the stars at night. One day we stopped, and had lunch in a small Mexican village. This is where I first dined on goat stew complete with bits of fur, cartilage, and vertebrae. Naturally I bought a bottle of tequila. I was very pleased that my age wasn't a concern in Mexico.

On a cliff jump one afternoon, I decided to drop out of college, and join the Marines because I was under the impression the Marines would be similar to this kayaking trip. And what's not to like about that?

That summer I went back to Cleveland, and cleaned up my act — knocking off the drinking and smoking. I talked to a Marine recruiter, and took the ASVAB, an assessment test. I scored high enough to do pretty much any military occupational specialty the Marine Corps had to offer.

I had no idea what job to do because I was under the misconception that all Marines pretty much went camping with guns in between traveling the world, and seducing foreign women. I thought tanks looked pretty aggressive, and considered being a tanker. My recruiter talked me out of that by showing me a poster of cool looking guys jumping out of planes, fast roping out of helicopters, and SCUBA diving.

"Yeah I wanna do that! What is it?"

"It's Recon, but you'll have to join the infantry first, and then take the screening. If you don't pass you'll be stuck in the infantry. Are you sure?"

"Yeah I wanna do that!" I thought the infantry sounded cool too.

To be clear, I had absolutely no idea what I was getting into. I just wanted to be a Marine, and "become a man."

By the time everything was in order it was fall, and I was scheduled to begin boot camp in Parris Island, SC on January 10, 2000. I began training a few times a week with the other recruits under the supervision of Bobby Fertell. I went to high school with him, and he'd joined the Corps right after. We would try to memorize the rank structure and general orders. Then we would run in formation around town chanting Marine cadence. It was great. I also ran, and did pull-ups and pushups on my own.

I was fairly uncertain of my physical abilities, and was anxious about it. Always questioning, "Will I make it?"

Both of my grandfathers had served in World War II. One in the Navy and one in the Army. Neither spoke of it more than to acknowledge that it had occurred (my family could be said to be a bit anti-social). But nonetheless, I knew they were proud of me for joining the Marines. My parents were proud as well. My dad took me to the fire station so one of his buddies could show me how to disassemble and assemble an M16. I felt well-liked; highly regarded, even. Right before I left for boot camp, my grandmother cooked me up a batch of her city chicken (breaded, fried pork cubes on a stick), and wrapped it in foil so I could take it with me.

I arrived at MCRD Parris Island on a bus packed with new recruits. It was night. The bus doors opened, and a Drill Instructor exploded in through the doors, barking in that bizarre, strained, Drill Instructor voice, "Get off of my bus! Do it now! Today! TODAY! Get off my bus! Do it now!" There was a stampede to disembark the bus.

Once outside, another Drill Instructor ordered us to form it up on the infamous yellow footprints. From there we marched to in-processing for paperwork, were issued uniforms, and got our heads shaved. Several recruits had raised moles on their heads. The "barber" shaved the moles right off. They looked like stunned lab rats with their freshly shaved bleeding scalps. I was assigned to 3rd Battalion, Alpha Company. There was not much sleep that first day.

The 3-month-long Marine Corps Recruit Training is designed to beat the nasty civilian out of you, and then mold you into a Marine. Men and women do not train together. You live in an open squad bay. The toilets are simply lined up across the floor with no stalls. Everything is to be done "Now! Today!" All recruits are referred to as "Recruit." There is a high importance placed on not being an individual or "doing your own thing," which "will get people killed." Customs, courtesies, and traditions are taught, studied, and rehearsed. Much of the time is dedicated to Close Order Drill. Marching and rifle maneuvers. I was terrible at marching, and often I was made to "play games" instead.

Marine Corps Drill Instructors claim to have more games than "Milton-freakin'-Bradley." Some of the most memorable include going back and forth through the squad bay, crawling over and under the racks. Sometimes under the mattresses as well. Swabbing the deck can wear you out. This involves putting your hands on a towel, and running back and forth through the length of the squad bay. They also loved to dump everyone's footlocker in the middle of the squad bay, and then make us sort it out under a tight timeline. Parris Island is infested with biting sand fleas. For a particularly grievous offense, the platoon would be ordered to mark time (march in place) on a sand patch to "stir em' up." Then we would stand at attention while the sand fleas feasted. If someone moved, which always happened, we would repeat the process.

Marine Corps boot camp has its own language. The overweight recruits were "fat bodies" and went to the "pork chop" platoon to lose weight. Issued glasses have thick frames, and are called "BCG," birth-control goggles. Recruits with glasses are called "Portals." All recruits are referred to as "nasty" or "disgusting." As the USMC is a department of the Navy, Navy terminology is used extensively. "Portals" are windows, "deck" is the floor, "head" is the bathroom, "bulkheads" are walls, "port" and "starboard" for left and right, and oddly, "scuttlebutt" is a rumor or a drinking fountain. Our books, which outlined customs, courtesies, and traditions, were known as "knowledge…" "Knowledge is power." And we learned discipline through pain.

During boot camp, I was often hungry and tired. The squad bay didn't have heating. It was a chilly South Carolina winter, and my whole platoon came down with "the crud," a gross, chunky sort of upper respiratory infection. I remember eating the white pulp off of orange peels for the extra nutrients it offered.

We cleaned our rifles in the evenings, a kind of family time. As we cleaned, a Drill Instructor would yell, "Scrub!" and we'd respond with "Harder, faster, Sir!" Eventually we went to the rifle range, and qualified with our M16s. We shot out to 500 meters with iron sights, which I still find impressive. As they say, "Every Marine is a rifleman." Near the end of boot camp, we did the newly established Crucible, a multi-day field training evolution involving ruck marching, hand-to-hand throw downs, and simulated attacks.

I graduated boot camp in March as a Private First Class (PFC), since I had some college credit. My parents and grandparents attended my graduation, and bought me a new pair of boots. I went home for my 10 days of boot leave. Then reported to Camp Geiger, NC for the School of Infantry (SOI). The first night, 3 Recon Marines showed up, and said they would be holding a screening the following morning. I arrived bright and early, ran the Physical Fitness Test (PFT, which consisted of running 3 miles within 18 minutes, 20 dead-hang pullups, and 100 crunches in 2 minutes), and did the swimming evaluation with the other Recon hopefuls. I was the only one to pass, and so, I got orders to Amphibious Reconnaissance School (ARS) in Little Creek, VA upon completion of SOI.

SOI is like an extension of boot camp with less drill, more weapons instruction, and more field time. We worked up to around a 17-mile ruck march. We also did rappelling, patrolling, and a bit of land navigation. We shot the small squad-sized machine gun.

One night, while showering after some time in the field, I pulled a blue-gray, thumb size, blood-filled tick out of my armpit. It left a stream of blood running down my ribs. I was toughening up.

After SOI, I checked into a training platoon in Little Creek, Virginia. Corporal Williams and Sergeant Bull supervised and trained us. An ARS class was in progress. The training platoon was supposed to prepare us for the next ARS class. We ran, swam, and carried sandbags around on our shoulders. I learned how to do crossovers, which involves swimming the width of the pool underwater, getting a breath or two on the other side, and repeating. We played underwater football with weights, which was more like underwater wrestling. I started out as a mediocre swimmer at best, but I was in shape and had heart. My swimming began to improve.

In between PT sessions, we didn't have a whole lot to do. There was certainly some debauchery. College parties. Fist fights in Virginia Beach. Girls. One night I got drunk and mouthed off to an older guy in the platoon named Larry Pownell. Larry was reportedly a Golden Glove Boxer, and I liked to antagonize him. We ended up wrapping sheets around our hands, and boxing each other in the common area. He threw one right down the pipe, crushing my nose. I walked it off, and had two black eyes for awhile. To this day, I still own a crunchy, crooked nose.

There were lot of names I would meet later on from that training platoon in Little Creek. A rowdy bunch of guys, and good Recon Marines.

Prior to actually going to ARS, the ARS instructors came, and tested our swimming ability. I was a borderline case. Chief Duncan, a large, intimidating, Navy Corpsman, and ARS instructor called me out. He made me swim boxes around the pool on my own for observation. Then he took me to the deep end. We tread water. He acted like he was drowning, grabbing me, and pushing me under. Then he emptied his lungs, and sank to the bottom. I dove down, pulled his big, limp, body up, and swam us to the edge of the pool. He said I frog-kicked on my side stroke, and I didn't go to ARS.

I was devastated. I had failed. Now what? I had been in the Marine Corps for under 6 months at this time, and had no idea what fate awaited me. All I knew was I did not like failing.

I went back to the barracks with the rest of the guys who had made it, and soon began training in the pool with some of the better swimmers. I worked on cross-overs, and swam laps, doing my best not to frog-kick on my side stroke. My hard work paid off. When my buddies went to ARS, I received orders to Basic Reconnaissance Course in California.

I grabbed my sea bag, containing all my worldly possessions, and flew across the country. In Coronado, CA I checked in to another training platoon. It was about a month until the next BRC class was to kick off. In the meantime, I was sent to Scout Swimmer Course. Scout swimmers usually work in pairs. We were trained to disembark a small, rubber Zodiac boat far enough out to sea to avoid detection, swim to shore, and conduct reconnaissance. The idea is report on beach conditions prior to the rest of the team coming ashore. This course mostly entailed finning in the ocean, and paddling the small Zodiac boats in and out of the California surf.

There were also some shenanigans south of the border in Tijuana. They had nightclubs that were $15 all you can drink. In one such establishment a

Mexican on roller skates skated up to you and poured tequila down your throat while blowing a whistle. The strip clubs in TJ were quite seedy, doubling as brothels.

When the Basic Reconnaissance Course class finally picked up, I was rarin' to go. The BRC is a grueling 13-week course, which covers land navigation, patrolling, and amphibious operations. Due to the physical and mental stress of the course, attrition is high.

We were issued gear. Rucksacks with a sandbag, Y-harnesses for carrying canteens and magazines, and sling ropes with a carabiner. The sling rope identified us as ropers, and was to be tied in a loop and worn over our shoulders at all times. It could also be tied into a harness for rappelling. We ran everywhere we went, carrying our loaded rucksacks.

We trained on the Naval Amphibious Base Coronado along side the aspiring Navy SEALS. There was an instant rivalry between the Marines and the sailors. Stealing their numbered helmets. Cutting them up in the chow hall line. Basic bullying.

The first part of BRC was mostly physical training, intended to weed out the weak. We ran with sandbags in our rucks, and often did the SEAL Obstacle Course, which was tough.

Then we moved on to Land Navigation through the mountains of San Mateo. The San Mateo Mountains are steep, named after the site of the highest battle during WWI. We camped out in the bush day and night, and covered many miles a day under weight, locating ammo cans. Each ammo can had a paper puncher with a specific pattern with which each Marine punched his card, proving he had, in fact, found that specific site.

I somehow developed an awful pus-filled heat rash on my legs. The pus made a distinct scent when I pulled down my pants to relieve myself, and it looked like my legs were rotting off. But I still managed to find my points, day and night, thus passing Land Nav.

I advanced to Patrol Phase, in which we worked in teams, applying our land navigation skills. The instructors enjoyed hitting you with tear gas and flash bangs, generally for falling asleep. About halfway through, one of the instructors gave my team an egg McMuffin, which he cut into 6 slices, one for each of us. Sharing this little slice of Egg McMuffin bonded us as a team. It certainly didn't satiate us, but we were a family and it helped further the notion that there was light at the end of the tunnel.

We patrolled for about 5 days with little to no food or sleep, and under constant stress. More than one Marine experienced hallucinations due to sleep deprivation. I distinctly remember a garden gnome walking up to me as I attempted to establish communications with the High-Frequency field radio. Someone walked off forgetting to take their rifle. That wasn't fun for anyone.

We advanced to Amphib, which, in my opinion, was the hardest part. As a team of 6, we carried 16-foot Zodiac rubber boats three miles one way, from the boat house to the beaches of Coronado. The boats were heavy. They included all our kit, and the steel deck plates. Sometimes instructors would climb into one of the boats, jumping from boat to boat as we carried them. We were promised that, if we could make it in under 30 minutes, the instructors would drive the boats to the beach the next day. Allegedly, we made the time on the last day. Watches were banned, so who knows.

During Amphi Phase, we used fins to swim long distances, in our cammies, towing our rucksacks, working up to over-the-horizon swims, so called because you cannot see the shore upon insert. We also learned to drive and navigate small boats using nautical charts. I enjoyed driving my boat to the buoys, which were usually covered with stinking, angry sea lions at night.

We got beat up trying to punch through the California surf using only paddles. As in surfing, timing the ebb and flow of the waves was essential. I picked up the rank of Lance Corporal, and immediately thereafter, decided I wanted to mouth off to a Lieutenant. Making waves.

I graduated BRC as a Lance Corporal, and was shipped to 3rd Recon Battalion in Okinawa, Japan. I checked in and immediately got set to work cleaning the barracks. This continued as a welcome message for 4 days with little to no sleep. Okinawa was a proving ground. A place to sharpen your teeth. We patrolled, drank, fought, and whored.

The jungle, or "The J," as it was called, was rugged, hot, steep, thick, and relentless. It turned us into a hard, cohesive unit.

Barracks 3535 will forever be ingrained in my memory. First Sergeant Tim, or "Willy T," when he wasn't around. And Colonel Gavin. Both tough as nails. They made men out of us.

First Sergeant Tim was a drinker. But he would also run 10 miles up and down hills in the heat of Okinawa. Ironically, he had no tolerance for alcohol-related incidents. An incident usually resulted in "putting on your flame suit and getting fucking burned." Loss of rank, confinement to the barracks, loss of pay.

"Let your conscience be your guide, and your ass be the scoreboard. Because if you pour gasoline over your head and light a match, it's gonna fucking hurt. Alright? Okay?"

I recall walking back to the barracks after a noon Friday formation, and being tackled by Colonel Gavin. He put his knee into the side of my head, and told me he could kill me. I agreed, and he let me go. The guy was real warrior. He had huge kettle bells in his office, and was a Judo master. He would often surprise and motivate us during battalion formations. Once he pulled out a sword, making the point that "killing a man makes you feel powerful, like the first time you drive it home in a woman." Another time he pulled out a knife, and said how we could "rip him limb from limb, and bury him on the beach, and it would be fair, but he would take a few of us with him." He wrote and recited a poem called "Men of the Forward Shadow" at the Marine Corps Ball. He had lunch with me, and told me he figured that some scumbag warrior like me was probably going to fuck his daughter. He seemed to be okay with it. Unfortunately, I didn't know his daughter. Probably too high falutin' for the likes of me, anyway.

Due to lack of female contact, there were times I frequented the "Buy me drinky" bars in Oki. These establishments generally involve paying $15 for a Philippina girl to drink tea, and call you "honey." Sometimes you got lucky, and were able to sneak them into the barracks. But mostly it was a tease and waste of money. I managed to contract clap of the yap, and thought I was going to die.

Okinawa was a 1-year duty station. I extended a year, and got to go to Airborne School in Fort Benning, GA with 13 other Recon Marines from 3rd Recon Battalion. In the Army, Airborne School is a given, while in the Marines it's a privilege. Airborne School is not physically demanding compared to many other military schools. We were excited to be back in the States after a year in Japan. In Georgia, we were like Indians free on the range with the girls and the booze.

We completed 3 weeks of training in Georgia, in preparation for our first jump. At about 0900 on the morning of our first jump, I had my parachute on, and had been inspected by the jump master. We were waiting to board the plane. Then an Airborne Instructor informed us that all flights had been cancelled, including ours. I thought it was some kind of Army mind-fuck. He turned on a TV, and I watched a plane fly into the twin towers. It was 9/11/2001. We got 96 hours of liberty, and partied in Atlanta. But nothing felt the same, nothing would be the same.

Within two weeks, Airborne School was completed, and I went back to Okinawa to be deployed on the 31st MEU, aboard the USS Essex. I spent about 6 months on and off ship at this time. Marines don't do much on-ship. Mostly cleaning guns, counting radios, and waiting to land somewhere for either training or liberty. Internet didn't really exist on-ship at that time. Time became arbitrary. Sleep, eat, work out, repeat. No day, no night. I read about 1,000 books, and played tons of chess and spades. I enjoyed throwing the trash overboard, but didn't like doing the platoon's laundry. We hit ports in Australia, Thailand, Singapore, Guam, and South Korea.

We did a beach landing with landing crafts on Iwo Jima. Then hiked up Mount Suribachi. It was awesome.

In South Korea, we did the sketchiest rope/rappel course I've ever been a part of. I remember walking out on a 200-foot-high jankety rope bridge construction, being thankful I didn't fall through the missing steps, and rappelling face first on a frayed rope out of a "hell hole."

In Thailand, we did jumps, and a jungle survival course with the Thai Recon Marines. There were girls waiting at the drop zone with beer for us. At the end of the survival course, the Thais brought out a wooden box filled with live cobras. The Thai Marines gave us a hip-pocket class on how to catch cobras. Then, one at a time, a cobra was released, and everyone in the platoon caught and killed one. Mine stood up and hissed. I grabbed it behind the head and by the tail, shook it, straightened it out, and cut its head off. I drained the blood into a water bottle full of rice whiskey. Then I cut the snake's heart out, popped it, and dropped it into the whiskey like a garnish. I drank, and felt the power.

Thailand also offered wonderful liberty. The port was too shallow for the Essex to dock. We climbed down the ladder on the side of the aircraft carrier, and boarded a local businessman's speed boat. He gave us Heineken and business cards for prostitutes, who were waiting on the pier. I visited the bridge over the River Kwai, and watched the kickboxing, which took place outside of most of the bars.

Back in Okinawa, my platoon did the MC-5 transition course. The MC-5 is a square parachute really designed for free fall, but equipped with a static line. Static lines connect part of the parachute to a cable on the inside of the plane. When you exit the aircraft the line pulls, and the parachute automatically deploys after 4 seconds, 7 with the MC-5. The idea was that we could do high-altitude, high-opening jumps, and fly a long distance, navigating with a compass board to a designated location. There were quite a few mishaps given that the MC-5 was larger than a traditional static-line parachute, it took longer to open, and we were jumping in higher, thinner air. On one jump, I flipped through the risers, and my arm got knotted in the suspension lines. My parachute halfway collapsed, and I began to spiral toward the earth. At about 2500 feet, I pulled the device to cut away my main parachute, and deploy my reserve. I was absolutely terrified as I dropped into free-fall for about 3 seconds, before my reserve parachute deployed.

When a Recon Marine left Okinawa, the tradition was to have a paddle party. His teammates would spend hours sanding, decorating, and wrapping a wooden boat paddle, reminiscent of the Marine Raiders in WWII. We would gather at "Recon Point" at night, and present the paddle to the lucky individual. We would sing "Here's to Brother Recon, Brother Recon who's with us tonight. He's happy. He's jolly. He ate shit by golly. Here's to Brother Recon, he's with us tonight!" Everyone eventually got drunk and fought each other. It was perfect. The intensity with which this tradition was followed was certainly unique to Okinawa, from what I saw.

In December of 2002, I left Okinawa after 2 years, with orders to 2nd Force Recon Company. I checked in over Christmas, so the barracks were vacant except for a few shady characters. When I met Buck in the barracks, he promptly stood up and shit his pants. Then he ground the shit into the floor with his boot. Right on.

After Christmas, 2nd Force was getting ready to go to the Middle East.

We boarded the USS Bataan, and steamed past the Rock of Gibraltar, through the Suez Canal, and landed in Kuwait. While on ship, we practiced a good deal of close-quarters combat. Getting ready for war. We also received our smallpox vaccinations aboard ship. The shots left a pus-filled blister on the shoulder. We were told not to rub the pus in our eyes. Naturally the showers, and shitters flooded. Pus soaked band-aids littered the head. I noticed the majority of the reserve unit in our berthing failed to bring shower shoes (flip-flops). They had to walk through the flooded head in their socks.

In Kuwait I was assigned to a platoon of 12 men: Dagger 01. We included a senior Navy Corpsman, an officer, 2 senior enlisted Marines, and strangely, an Army Special Forces guy, we nick-named Foghorn Leghorn, due to his aloof attitude. Fast Track was a Gunnery Sergeant, and undoubtedly in charge of the dirty dozen. The rest of the platoon seemed either to be coming off of recruiting duty, or boot Recon Marines such as myself.

In Kuwait, we trained. We drove our four IFAVs in formation across the open desert. IFAVs (Interim Fast Attack Vehicles) are Mercedes jeeps lacking windshields and doors. They are more narrow than a Humvee, allowing them to fit in the CH53 helicopter. Each IFAV had three men in it. Two had .50 caliber machine guns, and two had MK19s, a gun which fires 40-millimeter grenades at a cyclic rate, and has a tendency to jam. I was a driver. Driving at night through the Kuwaiti desert using night vision was a strenuous exercise. Machine guns, jeeps, and close quarters battle (CQB). We felt dangerous.

Jim Jamison and I, both Corporals at the time, made a habit out of surprise attacking, and wrestling to the ground, any cocky Staff Sergeant as a joke. In our free time, we would hang out by the females' port-a-shitters, cracking jokes and looking for action. We also filled a 5-gallon jug with apple juice, yeast, sugar, and honey pilfered from the chow hall. Eventually the concoction turned into drinkable "hooch," which we shared with the willing.

We lived in large tents. There once was an incredible sandstorm during which we were pretty well exposed; it filled all our equipment with talcum powder-like desert sand. Everyone ended up getting a sickness of the bowels. Jim managed to splatter liquid shit into his sweatshirt hood while running to a port-a-shitter. Periodically, "GAS GAS GAS!" was broadcast on a loudspeaker. This was the cue for us to don and clear our gas masks, and run to a bunker. We carried two auto-injectors filled with who-knows-what, allegedly designed to stave off the effects of gas if you were unlucky enough to inhale some. WMDs and all.

In mid-March, we camped out in the sand on the border of Kuwait and Iraq, dressed in our charcoal-filled, MOPP (Mission Oriented Protective Posture) suits under scud missile fire. MOPP suits are intended to neutralize the effects of chemical weapons as the command was concerned with chemical warfare. I thought it was stupid, and hated wearing my MOPP suit, but at least it provided some warmth. March in the Middle East is chilly, especially driving with no windshields. I was jealous of the Special Forces guys I saw. They looked like they were going deer hunting, wearing mismatched uniforms and cowboy hats. The artillery fire had kept me up most of the night. Light broke, and we invaded Iraq.

We were a part of Task Force Tarawa. Day One, we were tasked with conducting a reconnaissance mission along a main supply route on top of a levy dike. There were murals of Saddam Hussein on the road. Driving into the city of An Nasiriyah, local nationals stood outside of their homes giving us the thumbs down sign signal and/or slashing their hands across their throats. We drove on.

We eventually came upon a fortified Iraqi military establishment at the end of a street. A car sped past us, and turned. I think two Iraqis jumped out, and began shooting at us. Foghorn Leghorn was the first to jump into the street, and he started firing. This unleashed a barrage of heavy fire from the fort, and from our turret-mounted guns. Potsy, our lead vehicle driver, managed to launch a 40 mm grenade into the offending vehicle, while everyone else dumped rounds into that car. Machine guns were blazing on both sides. We began to take mortar fire. I jump out of the driver's seat, took a knee, and shot back. I remember seeing bullets skipping off the ground in front of me, but reality seemed to be moving in slow motion.

I aimed my M4 at muzzle flashes, emptying a magazine, and reloading. Jim unleashed his 40 mm machine gun. It jammed. Matt Richter, our vehicle commander, jumped over the roll cage and helped Jim fix it. We shot. They shot.

As we were only 12 men, we eventually had to break contact. I saw the lead vehicles turning around, so I stopped shooting, and jumped back into the driver's seat. I threw the IFAV into reverse, and dumped the gun truck over the levy dike from which we were fighting. I yanked the differentials, and drove the jeep up the steep dirt incline, back onto the road. Mortars pocketed the road as we drove away.

We drove back to "friendly lines," and debriefed. The Master Sergeant, who may or may not have been human, was shot through the pant leg, but otherwise we were unscathed. Adrenaline is a hell of a drug. Cherry popped! I wondered if this is what it would be like every day, and how long I could last.

Our reconnaissance patrol reportedly killed 25 Iraqi militants, and led the Marine Infantry in position to kill more. Word on the street was that they were afraid of the "little brown vehicles with the big guns."

I spent another restless night in the driver's seat, and in the morning drove into An Nasiriyah proper.

There were moments that I still remember clearly, and the rest of it seems to have blended together, with time and perception never quite matching up. I was a boot Recon Marine, which means I did what I was told to do, but was not let in on the overall game plan.

I remember pulling security in a truck outside of a hospital, while the Rangers rescued Jessica Lynch. I remember seeing Marine light-armored assault vehicles blown inside out on a street corner from friendly A-10 aircraft fire. I remember driving up to a bridge, and shaking hands with men I had been in Little Creek with. Meanwhile, a firefight took place a few hundred meters away. I remember seeing a US military truck with the driver's side door open with blood from its former occupant pooled on the seat, running into the street. I remember a night patrol in which we drove through "Ambush Alley" in order to escort ambulances full of wounded Marines back to friendly lines.

Tanks were a concern for us. Intel reported that the Iraqi Armored Division was up, running, and searching for Americans to kill. We were resting with a reserve recon unit in a semi-secure area, a concertina wire circle in the desert with our vehicles wagon wheeled, with the heavy guns manned and pointed outboard. Some wild-ass, reservist Gunnery Sergeant jumped onto the hood of his Humvee, and yelled "Incoming! Incoming!" A large vehicle was driving down the road just within view. Here come the tanks. Potsy ran into the street, took a knee, and began firing it up. As it got closer, I saw Iraqis jumping off the side of a shit-sucking truck, and running into the desert in order to escape the rifle fire. "Cease fire" was called. And we got on with the rest plan.

We stayed in and around An Nasiriyah for about a week. Then we began moving north in search of a mission to take out some of the playing-card-style high-value-targets. We were camped at an abandoned radio station, and caught wind of Chemical Ali, the maniac who gassed the Kurds, being holed up in the basement of the hospital in Al Diwaniyah. There was maybe 15 minutes of planning and preparation. We climbed into the back of a 7-ton, and were dropped off in front of the hospital in question. It was broad daylight.

We moved into the basement of the hospital, and began clearing rooms. As most of the doors were locked, we breached them by shotgunning the locks. Our twelve-man stack ended up splitting in order to clear more rooms faster. While clearing the furnace room, I became the front man. I turned a corner, and faced the other part of our stack, led by Fast Track. Thankfully, we both yelled the running password, "Devil Dog! Devil Dog! Devil Dog!" And continued our clearing.

Finally, an orderly ran down stairs with a key, and indicated he would open the doors rather than us continuing to shotgun the locks. We put him in front of the stack, pushed him into the rooms first as a sort of human shield, entering right behind him. One of the rooms contained a large number of stainless steel cabinets. Fast Track told the orderly to open the doors one by one, as we checked inside. After about the second cabinet the orderly opened a door directly into his forehead, fell to the ground, and started convulsing. Fast Track said, "He's faking it." And stomped his nuts. He continued to convulse, was carried out by another orderly, and we resumed shotgunning doors. Ultimately, we went back to the radio station without locating Chemical Ali.

We drove around a lot, looking for action, conducting reconnaissance and everything. We often spent nights in the desert, sleeping under our vehicles or in abandoned buildings. Fast Track had a pretty good supply of whiskey coming in the mail. At night we would share a drink or two. There was also a time when an Iraqi approached us on a street corner, and asked if we wanted whiskey. "Yes!" Jim and I replied with enthusiasm. He opened the trench coat he was wearing, revealing his wares. We paid him some American dollars, and drove away. It was like a movie.

The whiskey was called "Ranger." The label depicted a cowboy roasting a can of beans. The cap was definitely not sealed, and there was some kind of sediment floating in the liquor. We saved it until we met up with Buck Rammer, the floor shitter, and a friend in another platoon. Then we strained it through a sock, and split it three ways.

One of Fast Track's favorite activities was locating and destroying munition caches, and Iraqi weaponry. He would very methodically build a charge out of C4, and use it to blow up anti-aircraft guns and whatever other contraband he could find. One time we found a large munition cache in a field. There were needles and gas masks scattered about. Fast Track was like a kid on Christmas, daisy chaining the unexploded ordnance together. When his masterpiece went high order it released a small mushroom cloud of white smoke over the field. Then secondary detonations began to occur, firing rockets and mortars willy-nilly. A field may have unintentionally been set ablaze.

Another time we had to drive across a bridge covered with chanting, protesting Iraqis. Lopez, one of the other drivers, pulled his .45 out, and put it under his leg. In the process the pistol discharged into his seat. Everyone on both sides seemed to completely ignore this gun shot. We continued to drive across the bridge, through the crowd, and they continued to yell and shake their fists in protest.

On another bridge over a river, we pulled up to a stop as a crane was pulling a Marine tank out of the water. The story was it had driven over the side at night in a sandstorm. There were no survivors.

We received orders to move up to Al Kut, and establish linkup with the rest of the command. En route, there were abandoned Iraqi fighting holes dug in beside the road. As we were cruising down a main supply route, "Contact left" was called out over the radio. I looked, and saw Iraqi tanks with their cannons pointing directly at us. Immediately I swung the IFAV around, and proceeded to break contact, as per SOP. Fortunately, it turned out that the tanks were abandoned as well. I think Fast Track tried to call an air strike on them, but they wouldn't do it.

Driving through Iraqi villages, many of the people were happy to see us, and hailed us as liberators. "George Bush number one!" was a common slogan. Still, Jim and I felt powerful, and enjoyed pointing our guns at people.

In Al Kut, we linked up with the rest of 2nd Force Recon Company, which, for some reason, had been tasked out to 1st MEF. We managed to get cots, and slept in an abandoned airplane hangar. Instead of eating MRE's constantly, we occasionally got "tray rats," which are the military's field-expedient version of catering, a slight step up from MRE's if only for the sake of variety.

We went into Al Kut proper in a show of force to some protesting Iraqis holed up in an abandoned police station. They were chanting "NO, NO, CHALABI" referring to the Iraqi politician Ahmed Chalabi. They didn't have weapons or shoot at us so there wasn't much we could do.

We ended up getting tasked with a weapons interdiction mission on the Iraq/Iran border. It was believed that there was an underground network, funneling weapons from Iran to Iraq outside of Al Kut. Over the course of our time in and around the area, we captured a few bad guys, sporting fedayeen tattoos or taking pot shots at us. They were usually flex-cuffed with a sand-bag over their head, roughed up a bit, and sent away for interrogation.

We were tasked to go out into the desert for four days in order to conduct reconnaissance on what were thought to be weapon supply routes. Potsy had diarrhea, and stayed back in our hangar. He was told to guard the mortar tubes, RPGs, and other foreign weapons we had acquired.

The 11 of us went out for 4 days, driving around, observing, stopping cars, generally looking for trouble. We got skunked. Upon return to the hangar, Potsy was nowhere to be found. And worse, all our foreign weapons and war trophies were gone. Fast Track lost it: "Someone find me fucking Potsy!" Eventually

Potsy came waltzing back into the hangar, and Fast Track told him to pull his shit off the truck because he's out of the platoon. As Potsy was doing so, Fast Track continued to chew him out. Potsy had enough. He countered, "Fuck you old man, and your widow maker missions!" Then he kicked Fast Track in the face while standing on the back of the truck. They began sparring in the middle of the hangar. Fast Track trying to do some crazy spin kick, and Potsy boxing. The captain broke it up. After a cool down period the two Marines kissed and made up. Though we never recovered the treasures, Potsy was back in good graces.

My platoon did not get involved in the push to Baghdad. After the powers-that-be decided we were done in Al Kut, we made our way back to Kuwait for demobilization. I came down with some sort of allergic reaction, and couldn't stop sneezing. I sneezed incessantly, all day, every day. I sneezed until my chest and throat felt like they were coming apart. After about a week, it finally passed, and I was fine.

Someone gave us first-class seats on a plane back to the States. We were treated like heroes. I think we got back to Camp Lejeune, NC in the end of May or early June of 2003.

Back in the States, I got a little out of control with my drinking, fighting, and carousing. I was used as a battering ram, and literally thrown out of a strip club head first. I almost burned it down with a cup of gasoline, and blood dripping off my chin. The cops showed up outside, and I caught a cab instead.

Another time I took a full champagne bottle to the side of the head, blacked out, and came to with the culprit's blood up to my elbows. My vision was skewed for a week or two. I got beat up by the military police for mouthing off, drunk. In a parking lot, a chick slapped me until my ears rang. I pushed her down, the bar cleared, a gun was pulled, and a railroad tie was swung. I suffered minor repercussions from the command. But it was mostly swept under the rug.

When I was considering my next move in life, the story I remember hearing back at the company was that we had won the war, and we might go back to Iraq the next year for peacekeeping operations. I wasn't into it. I wanted to try life on my own as a former Marine.

At 24, I quickly lined up a job, which paid six figures. In January 2004, I got out of the Marines, and went to work as a security contractor in Afghanistan, protecting the US Ambassador.

To be honest, I wish I had stayed in for another enlistment. There were no peacekeeping missions the following year. Only battles like Fallujah in which friends of mine fought and died, while I watched it on the news in Afghanistan. I wished I had been there with them. I still do.

My 4-year Marine Corps enlistment seems like a stroke of luck. I managed to be in the right place, at the right time, most of the time. I never quit, and always gave it everything I had. This allowed me to advance fairly high in a relatively short amount of time.

In the end, I probably needed a mentor, and most likely could still use one. I spent the years from 2004-2012 working in Iraq and Afghanistan as a security contractor. It started off great, and slowly became more like a high-paying dead-end job. But that's another story though.

At this point in time I'm still in a transitional period. I'm trying to figure out how and if I fit into society.

Semper Fidelis. ✧

My name is Nathaniel Lobas. Some people know me as Pete. After attending the Basic Reconnaissance Course, I began my military career at 3rd Reconnaissance Battalion in Okinawa, Japan in 2000. I attended the Urban Reconnaissance and Surveillance Course and Airborne School in order to support the 31st MEU, aboard the USS Bataan (LHD-5). On the 31st MEU, my platoon trained in Thailand, Australia, Guam, South Korea, and Singapore. Highlights of this deployment include a mock beach landing and hike up Mount Suribachi, Iwo Jima, and catching, beheading, and drinking the blood of cobras during a Thai Jungle Survival Course.

After 2 years in Okinawa, I rotated to 2nd Force Reconnaissance Company in December 2002. Shortly after checking in, I was issued gear, began CQB training with my new platoon, and boarded the USS Essex en-route to Kuwait. My Force Recon platoon were among the first Americans to enter Iraq in March 23, 2003. We fought in the Battle of An Nasseriya, and were involved in the Jessica Lynch rescue. We worked our way to Al Kut, and ran weapons interdiction missions on the border of Iraq and Iran.

I ended my tour of duty with the Marine Corps as a Sergeant in January 2004, and soon found employment protecting the US Ambassador in Afghanistan as a private contractor. I worked in Iraq and Afghanistan from 2004-2012 for a variety of different government agencies and companies. Some of the more noteworthy locations I worked in include Basra, Ramadi, Baghdad, Kirkuk, Kabul, Kandahar, and Herat.

Since 2012, I have been attending school in order to become a civil engineer. I am employed as a part-time consultant for Invictus Security. This position sends me to natural disaster zones around the world, such as Nepal and Beirut, in support of programs providing humanitarian aid. ✦

nlobas11@hotmail.com

Chris Lyke

Tuesday's Gone

When I was a kid, the Challenger blew up on television. We were all sitting in the school library, watching man's latest grasp for the heavens when something went wrong, an O-ring here or there, and I thought that that was it: the moment that I'd never forget. I remember how it looked on the television, and how, when it began to burst and tumble and disintegrate before our adolescent eyes, none of us were sure what was happening. It was so foreign to our post-WWII "perfectam vitae" that, as it turns out, none of us could accept that something was wrong. We watched it all unfold, publicly, and suspended our disbelief until our teachers started freaking out. Then the collective, Midwestern, empathetic sobbing started and, like I said, it had to be the moment I'd remember forever, like how my folks talked about the President getting killed in '63. Obviously, I was premature.

By September of 2001, I'd been teaching English on the south side of Chicago for a year or two. Derrick, a squirrely ne'er-do-well of a junior, burst into the classroom that Tuesday morning yelling, "They're blowing up the buildings! They're blowing up New York!" It was then that I knew the old marker, the old gold standard of national tragedy, had been obliterated. From here on out, the world would be new, and dangerous. In a way, the old versions of us all have been stuck there, in that high school classroom, ever since. It was as if our old lives ended there.

Unlike many soldiers, I didn't join until I was thirty-one. I'd had an entire first act, and even a second act, before I raised my hand for Uncle Sam.

This story starts long before that Tuesday in September; it starts a few decades earlier, in Ohio. Most of my childhood was spent in the woods southeast of Cleveland. Our backyard ended where the forest began, and for an eight-year-old, it was unending and dense and beautiful. It's where our summers were spent. My sister and I lived a childhood that was nearly the same as that of our parents' generation. We played outside. We rode around in Fords and Chevys that took leaded gas and shimmied and trembled when driven over fifty-five. We climbed trees, swam in the creek, messed around with crayfish, and rabbits, and snakes. We played World War Two with the neighbor boys: the woods outside of the little one-floor ranch house became a bloodless Ardennes, or Hurtgen Forest. We acted out the episodes of Batman and Robin, Star Trek, and Combat with Vic Morrow. That place, in the 1970s, was close to perfect for a little boy. Above all else though, we played sports, incessantly, and in Ohio, it was football.

Some people think of high school and shudder. I do not. Like anyone's teenage years, there were bad times, but I had competent teachers and some great friends. My grades were average, but I had high test scores. Mostly though, high school was about the football team. Dedication to that rough sport gives a young person all the tools needed to succeed in a work environment or, as it turns out, the infantry. Being able to get your tail kicked around and still perform in the heat, and then in the cold, sometimes with injuries, and even being accepting of the occasional loss are lessons that team sports teach. Especially football, with its violence and rough play, goes a long way in preparing a young person for life after school. This is not the only way, but this way worked for us.

I finished high school in '90, played a good enough linebacker that it got me into college, and off I went: handsome, youthful, and utterly oblivious. I was a casual student that should have studied archeology, or at least history, but I'd snagged an English degree because it was easy to maintain solid grades. By the beginning of my freshman year, I'd quit the football team – they weren't paying my way anyhow – and picked up the guitar. I had decided that pursuing music was to be my real passion, and I couldn't be bothered by difficult classwork. In true punk-rock fashion, the boys in the adjoining dorm rooms loved music, could barely play themselves, and wanted to write songs and play in a band. The second act began.

We wrote songs and we learned how to play. We played anywhere that would take us. We'd drive to Cleveland or Toledo to go on at nine o'clock on a Wednesday to an empty bar. It didn't matter, we were getting better, we were getting serious and over time, things started to change. The next few years saw some success: seven-inch records, cassettes and CDs, battles of the bands, and local tours.

By '95 we'd graduated from college and done the circuit in Ohio. Dayton had become a little too small for us, so we decided to choose between Chicago and New York. We'd spent a couple long, fantastical weekends in Chicago, including a Paddy's Day or two. We'd met girls and other bands and had gotten along well. So that was it, the decision was made: we'd stay in the Midwest and move to Chicago. The biggest chip-on-the-shoulder town in the world.

Despite living in a rough part of town, with a whorehouse for a neighbor and a seemingly unending cast of criminals selling drugs across the street, we were happy and focused in our new city. We were young and without responsibility, in a cheap apartment, only a few blocks west of the bars and restaurants and venues of Wicker Park. We were firmly seated in the bubble of the nineties. There was no longer a Soviet threat, and there were jobs just lying around. The president was listening to Fleetwood Mac and had even played a bad saxophone on late night TV. The 1890s are sometimes referred to as the "Gay 90s," or the "Gilded Age." The 1990s, a century later, could also be said to have that careless, and carefree, go for broke élan that typified American and European cities prior to the inferno of the First World War. My friends and I — mothers and fathers, and middle-aged now —sped around the Midwest from festival to party to festival, always back to Chicago, temping in offices and creating art based on happiness and catharsis. Without a real bogeyman to combat, there was also a fair bit of self-loathing. (It needs to be said that this self-loathing was most often of the garden variety, borne out of the sticker shock of looming adulthood.) It was mostly beautiful art though, and beautiful thought, and study, all the while wearing the affected cloak of "Generation X."

I disparage it now, but was firmly embedded in that world when it was happening. We were daring on the trapeze swings, but there was definitely a net. We had no idea what was coming. The economy and the lack of a real existential threat made us skew towards the fanciful, the psychedelic, and the dreamer.

Eventually Chicago sends one the bill. The city, and its violence, and price, and winter, and packs of roving, wild dogs in Humbolt Park alleys swallowed us up. Hindsight says we should have stayed in Ohio, getting a bigger following and living on the cheap. But by the end, with day jobs grinding us down, and success eluding us yet again, things just kind of fell apart. The band was on its last legs. The drummer moved to Brooklyn, and bankruptcy and debt loomed larger than the skyline.

In Chicago, the sun comes up over the lake and then over the skyscrapers, casting bizarre and jagged shadows across the rest of the city every morning. It was something one looked forward to seeing. By '99 it reminded us only of our miniscule size, and monstrous failure. It brought to light the reality of running in place in the shade and created a very real and constant sense of dread and forfeit.

I suppose I should have gotten a law degree to pay for everything, but a girl in a bar told me about a one-year teaching program at DePaul University that started paying right away. I enrolled. Besides, although the music was teetering, I didn't want anything as serious as law school to divert my attention from riding that sinking ship to the bottom of the sea.

By '01, the band was done, the drummer was gone, we'd turned thirty (gasp), and I was in a classroom on the south side of Chicago teaching British Lit. And this is when, that Tuesday morning, young Derrick stormed into my classroom giving us all the horrifying news. The bubble of the nineties had burst, and we could suddenly see the enemy backing away slowly, and then disappearing, as we picked ourselves up off the floor and put towel to nose.

I walked into the recruiting office at Addison and Western. The recruiter tested me and I scored fairly high. He started listing off all the different jobs I could get but I only wanted one. I told him that I'd enlist for four years as an infantryman and that I'd like to go to boot camp at some point after the school year ended. He shrugged, told me I had to lose five pounds, and we started on down the paper trail, getting everything in order. I wound up heading down to Ft. Benning in early September and, because it was the fall, thoroughly enjoyed the Georgia weather, and boot camp. There wasn't much sleep, and we exercised constantly, but at the end of the day it was a process without any wasted time. The army has the system of turning civilians into soldiers down to a science. My college psychology classes were full of theory and empirical, though impersonal, data. Down there at infantry school I watched the Drill Sergeants employ many of these ideas. There's a good chance they weren't familiar with the big names in the field, but they were clinical in the use of rewards and punishments, and positive and negative reinforcement. I watched chubby eighteen year olds from Wisconsin and Texas turn lean, and focused, and with gritted teeth marched alongside them on fifteen-mile marches: field problems, rifle ranges, bivouacs, and "standing to" just before the sunrise. To my surprise I was a pretty good shot and, probably because of age and experience, led most of the patrols as a squad leader. Later, when I became an actual sergeant, and a squad leader, I realized it was easily the best job I'd ever had.

Several years and two deployments later I found myself walking uphill, over the rocks and broken shrubbery that did its best to lessen the beauty of the Afghan mountains. This situation, patrolling to pick a fight with Pashaii tribesmen, was an escalation borne of another tragedy, this one inflicted upon us by other human beings rather than caused by an faulty gasket. We were there for vengeance, and this fact was imprinting an even bigger calamity on those involved than the exploding spaceship and its martyred crewmen.

I got home, and then out of the Army, in '09. It's only after six years of civilian life, and the memory of countless patrols, that I see the futility in the time we spent over there. I'm not saying it was all folly. It wasn't for nothing, I mean. After all, we succeeded on a daily basis: passing out human assistance to villagers in an effort to curry favor, or patrolling up and down the tiny stone and dirt roads in an effort to keep them clear of the enemy. We walked untold miles up and down the Mayl Valley, getting shot at enough to know what it's all about. We woke up in the middle of the night as rockets slammed into our mountain outpost and machine gun fire zipped by just above our heads, firing back into the blackness of that unpowered night at muzzle flashes. We watched our mortars blast the rocks and then we walked out looking for body parts. We guarded up-ended American vehicles for days fending off the probes and creepers trying to get a PR victory by pushing us off the site. We were successful in these things. But upon the last American's departure, the Taliban, whomever we decide they are, will be strolling right back in. In some way or other, Kabul will fall.

I'm back in the classroom now, and a lot has happened since the last time I taught. The Army, the war, a marriage, and fatherhood have all happened. I got out of the service. I wanted to raise my kids and to be with them, alive and in one piece. I wanted to see them grow and live and hopefully make fewer mistakes than I've made. When I left, my daughter was old enough to pine for her daddy. Overseas, I got an unending supply of crayon-drawn love-notes from my four-year-old. When I got home, there was emotion and joy and she rarely left my side. My son, on the other hand, was born in between deployments. He turned three a couple months before I got home from Afghanistan. He didn't know who I was, despite seeing pictures, and was terrified of being alone with me, even though my wife consoled him. It took him a good year and a half to start really trusting me. It was a difficult time.

Coming home has provided a whole different set of challenges, too. The problem, despite being told incessantly that you're going to be changed, and awkward, and angry, is that one doesn't realize the change. One feels normal and cannot see anything but the same old mug in the mirror. It's a bit like being surrounded by a wildfire and not knowing it. It's as though everything is burning up around you, the floorboards and beams are set alight, lattice work burning away, but it's imperceptible. The civilities and niceties, the social safeguards and manners and checks and balances that keep one surviving in the modern American world have been burned away and replaced with quick twitch reflexes, spidey-sense, and a hyper-aggressiveness that is only one traffic jam or crowded train car away from coming to the fore.

The version of you that is requisite in order to survive, and succeed, overseas is in some ways the "best" you. It is the most feral and close to nature. Old Freud talked about these gifts from our ancestors – these genetic responses and the ability to do great harm – that we suppress and block and forego in order to live in a safe society and raise our families. Those are the floorboards and timbers that were burned away by the war. All that gets left are fake-building storefronts, plywood and held up by planks like the movie sets of days gone by. Those façades could be destroyed by a child, let alone a city like Chicago.

The beat poet Lew Welch said Chicago was a, "great, red rhinoceros, stamping its feet" along the shores of Lake Michigan. "It's already running us down." He said. That beast can be hard on one's psyche if that mental state is plywood and flimsy and starting to crack. The old magic that had kept me youthful and honest and upstanding had gone, and except for driving the kids to soccer, or making dinner for my wife, I was really a defrocked monk, or better yet, Merlin, banished to the cave for not being able to cast a spell to save his life.

So that's where I found myself two years after getting home. The early problems of reintegration: the inability to drive (imagine pointing machine guns at anyone who nears your vehicles and a week later trying to drive in the Chicago Loop at rush hour), or the inability to speak to anyone in a civil manner. I found myself saying "fuckin' grande, please" to the girl behind the counter at Starbucks. And of course, there's the drinking. Hitting it hard at noon and passing out on the sidewalk at Division and Hoyne by two-thirty, while the kids sat in pre-school. Trying to keep from crying at a party because something random reminded me of a dead child, or shattered legs, or handless, bleeding Pashai fighters shot through the face and still running to find a place from which they'd try to kill more Americans.

These ghosts, brought back from overseas, stay with us. Our own personal Jacob Marleys. Sometimes, usually through staying busy, we're able to keep them from rattling the chains outside the door. This works for a while. But despite my busy schedule, there were cracks in the façade and a shapeless, undefined desire to do something about it began to occupy my thoughts. After getting together with a friend I'd been overseas with, a fellow writer, an idea formed that has given some purpose to my dwindling free time. We talked at length about a venue for veteran arts and literature. Not necessarily a place for guys to tell war stories, those exist in abundance, but rather an arty online magazine for vets.

Writing, talking, thinking about one's experiences has a way of exorcising the ghosts for a lot of veterans. That was the idea at least. After a couple more meetings, we decided to start lineofadvance.org. We raised money and hired designers and got the site up and running. It's moved forward in fits and starts, but has given a voice to veterans and the families of veterans. It's introduced me to a real fraternity of veteran writers and artists that stretches all throughout the country. Our work continues to pop up in different magazines or online collections and, because of this network, we're able to help one another with advertising, promotion, and often just an ear from someone who's been there.

Things are always getting better. Family, and art, and especially my children, re-centered and have re-grounded my psyche. It's helpful to have something more important than oneself to pull you from anger and the terrible thoughts that many of the men and women have upon getting home. This, and time, have helped me with further reintegration. Time has dulled the violence, and the fear, and allowed the old, civilian version of myself to re-emerge. Six years after getting home, a fourth act has begun. A fourth act filled with chances to be taken, bold choices, fatherhood, creativity, and a belief in the future. ✧

Christopher Lyke served in the U.S. Army from 2003-2010 as an enlisted infantryman. He has a Master's degree in Education from DePaul University and works as a teacher in Chicago. He also runs Line of Advance, a non-profit website for veteran art and writing. On Saturdays in the fall, he can be found watching the Buckeyes at Vaughn's Pub. Chris has been published in Blaze Vox, Proud To Be Vol. 4, and Military Experience and the Arts. ✦

www.lineofadvance.org

chris@lineofadvance.org

William Pat Tyree

Prologue

"Hey Nav! I need a heading to get us clear of this weather!"

The pilot's voice was nervous and agitated inside my headset.

"Pilot. Nav. Fly heading 310. We'll clear the weather in two minutes," I replied, and started counting the seconds.

One second. Two seconds. Three seconds.

At fifteen seconds, the pilot rolled out on heading 310. Ten seconds after that, I radioed AWACS.

"Sentry-Three-Zero. Guppy-One-One."

"Guppy-One-One. Sentry-Three-Zero. Go ahead."

"Guppy-One-One is bulls-eye two-seven-zero at three-five miles, heading three-one-zero at flight level two-two-zero. Request to move Ruby anchor point northwest 15 miles to stay clear of weather."

"Guppy-One-One cleared as requested."

The date was Tuesday, March 5th, 1991. We were flying our umpteenth air refueling sortie in support of Operation Desert Storm. Today the Air Tasking Order had us scheduled to rendezvous with a couple of EF-111s over southern Iraq. Although the hostilities had ended five days earlier, there were still aircraft flying scheduled patrols, and as long as there were aircraft flying, they needed fuel to stay aloft.

Inside the thunderstorm, the air was filled with turbulence and static electricity. The tanker shook violently as it passed through columns of rapidly rising and falling air. St. Elmo's fire crawled up the windscreens. Then came a bright flash followed by a tremendous "BOOM!" as St. Elmo leapt off our aircraft and discharged into the cloud ahead of us.

I took a deep breath and looked around. We were still flying. I realized that the 100,000 pounds of fuel we were carrying had not exploded into a massive fireball. Too late. My bowels felt like they'd dropped through the bottom of the aircraft's fuselage and were left dangling there for all the world to see.

Ninety seconds. Ninety-one seconds. Ninety-two seconds.

I peered into the radar scope and saw the electronic reflection of the EF-

111s ten miles to the northeast. I correctly assumed that the AWACS controller was talking to them on a different frequency.

"Guppy-One-One. Sentry-Three-Zero. Your receivers will be contacting you on A-R frequency momentarily." It was almost as if the AWACS controller was reading my mind.

"Guppy-One-One" was my only response.

Moments later, the lead pilot of the EF-111 flight chimed in. "Guppy-One-One. Raven-Two-One. Flight of two. Angels-Twenty-One. Nose cold. Two-Nine-Nine-Two set." The lead pilot was telling me there were indeed two aircraft and that they were 1,000 feet below me at 21,000 feet. Their weapons systems were on standby and their altimeters were set to the standard setting for flights above 18,000 feet.

"Raven-Two-One. Guppy-One-One. Roger. You are cleared to position your flight one mile in trail. Maintain two-one-thousand feet."

One-Hundred-Ten seconds. One-Hundred-Eleven. One-Hundred-Twelve. Five miles southeast of the repositioned anchor point, we broke out of the clouds and into a large patch of clear night air.

We maintained our northwest heading until the receivers were in pre-contact position. Then I directed the pilot to fly east-west legs of 20 miles to keep things easy. In the short span of ten minutes, we completed the refueling and our receivers were headed back north to their assigned patrol area.

I contacted AWACS. The controller cleared us off station to return to base at FL330. As we climbed to our assigned altitude, I asked myself: *Why? Why are we still doing this? Why are we still hanging our collective ass on the line when the shooting war has ended? Why? Why? Why?*

We were all proud to say we did our part to save the world from Saddam Hussein. Now that our job was done, did it make sense to send us back into the sky each day? What was the value of a combat support mission when the combat was effectively over? Another fun-filled sortie like this one and our families might be greeting flag-draped coffins – that is, if the Search and Rescue teams were lucky enough to find us.

Early Years

My name is William Patrick Tyree, Pat for short. I come from a family steeped in military history. My great-great-great-great-great-grandfather, James Tyree, served as a Lieutenant in the Virginia militia during the American Revolution. My great-grandfathers fought on opposing sides during the Civil

War. My dad was a bomber pilot during WWII and again during the Korean conflict. He had a 35-year career with the Illinois Air National Guard, and it rubbed off on me.

My earliest childhood memories are family vacations to Michigan, when my dad's air guard unit deployed to Alpena County Regional Airport for two weeks each summer. We stayed at Legere's Resort on nearby Long Lake. While dad and his colleagues trained for war, mom caught up on her reading and watched us swim in the frigid lake waters.

During the middle weekend of the trip, dad's unit sponsored an open house. They invited the servicemen's families out to the airport for a tour of the facility and a summer barbecue. It was on one of those open-house tours that I saw my first jet airplane up close and personal.

It was 1959; I was four years old. I recall walking with my dad near one of the hangars. There were a few F-86 fighters on static display. He asked me if I wanted to see the inside of one of them. For me that meant climbing up a rickety set of portable metal stairs and I shook my head *no*!

We walked along for a time until I spied a brand new T-37 Tweet. The airplane was small, low to the ground and I could see into the cockpit with relative ease.

I told my dad, "I like this plane. One day I'm going to fly it." He told me that he believed I would.

From that day forward, all I could think of was flying airplanes. I'd lay on my back in the yard and watch the airplanes fly south on their departure routes out of O'Hare International Airport in Chicago. I asked my dad questions like what I had to do to get to fly. He said that I had to study hard and get good grades in school, and above all, I had to have good eyesight. He said that the Air Force wanted pilots with "eagle eyes."

I did my best to study hard and get good grades. No matter how hard I studied, the fact remained that I had inherited my mom's eyesight and not my dad's. Mom had myopia and her vision was something like 20/400. I watched as each of my siblings required glasses by the time they were 8.

Each year in grade school, the nuns would lead us into the school basement for our annual hearing and vision tests. I passed the vision test through seventh grade. Then one day, Sister Joseph Ann caught me squinting at the chalkboard from my seat at the rear of the classroom. She told me to exchange seats with a student seated at the front of the class. In the seconds it took me to move to the head of the class, my dream of ever becoming a pilot evaporated.

Sister Joseph Ann called my mom and told her about my squinting. When I returned from school that day, my mom had already made an appointment with the eye doctor. Later that evening, as we watched Chet Huntley and David Brinkley report on the war in Vietnam, I asked my dad if I could ever be a pilot if I wore glasses.

He said that it was OK if you needed to wear glasses after you completed pilot training, but that the Air Force wanted all their new pilots to have 20/20 vision. I sulked. My heart was broken. Dad must have noticed because he added that I could still become a navigator. It was a bargaining chip. Dad wanted to give me a sliver of hope, but the damage was done. I would never be a pilot.

I slogged through high school. My sophomore year report cards were not stellar and my attitude toward school was equally low.

"You are not working to your true potential," my dad would sternly remind me. He was now a Lieutenant Colonel in the Illinois Air Guard. It was about this time that my mom and her friends began volunteering their time at an office in downtown La Grange. Their goal was to help young men of draft age seek legal deferments.

When mom informed dad about what she and her friends intended to do, it set the stage for several days of dinner table theatrics. Every evening at 6:00, dad would turn on the evening news. It didn't help that the news emanated from a 13-inch Motorola portable television situated on a tabletop in the corner of our home's dining room.

Every evening as the body count numbers were reported, my mom would ask dad if he was aware that each of their three sons would one day be of draft age.

Each evening dad's answer was the same. "Yes, dammit! I know!"

There wasn't anything dad could do to stop the war in Vietnam, nor was there anything he could do to stop the growing flow of American young men into that far-off region. There was, however, something he could do to appease his wife and reduce the risk of his sons one day coming home in body bags. There was a way their sons could serve honorably in the military and avoid being drafted into service. Toward the end of my second year of high school, I submitted an application for entry into the Illinois Air National Guard and completed the USAF airman qualifying examination. Then I forgot about the whole deal and pursued an interest shared by all my friends – girls.

I graduated high school on Friday, June 9th, 1972. My folks left for vacation with my younger sister the next day. The following Monday, I was seated at the table eating lunch with my girlfriend when the phone rang.

"This is Tech Sergeant Jon Philips with the Illinois Air National Guard at O'Hare. May I speak with William Tyree?"

I'm not usually called William. In fact, my first driver's license was issued to one Patrick W. Tyree. It took me a moment to figure out that the guy on the phone wanted to speak with me.

"This is he," I said, wondering what this was all about.

"William, your name was selected for enlistment into Illinois Air National Guard as an Avionics Repair Technician and you are scheduled to report for basic military training at Lackland Air Force Base on July 9th." Jon paused.

Things were happening fast. "Yes…" was my puzzled response.

"William, I need to know verbally if you will accept our offer."

My head was spinning and I asked, "When do you need to know?"

"If you don't say yes, we will dispose of your application and call the next man on the list. Believe me, there are plenty."

I looked at my girlfriend and turned away. Then I spoke into the phone with the most controlled voice I could muster, "Yes. I accept. What do I do now?"

Jon informed me that I had to meet with him at the base personnel office the next day and complete my paperwork. He said that I would have some forms to bring home and get signed by one of my parents since I was not yet eighteen.

Jon finished the call by saying that since I wasn't leaving for basic training for another few weeks, I could schedule my swearing-in any time before July 9th.

I thanked him, then hung up the phone and looked at my girlfriend. I walked over to the table and sat across from her. Then I told her that I had agreed to enlist for six years.

Her response was utter disbelief. "Just like that?"

"Just like that," was my response.

She couldn't believe that I committed the next six years of my life at the drop of a hat. I assured her that this was another step in a plan that started two years ago, and that I'd be away in training for 36 weeks and would return as a civilian soldier for the remainder of the six years. In truth, although "the plan" was in the works for the last two years, in fact I, too, was shocked that I'd committed. In the short span of a two-minute phone conversation, the wheels of fortune were placed in motion.

The next few weeks were a whirlwind of activity. My family, mostly my mom, helped me make preparations for my departure. My friends were curious to know where I was going, what I'd be doing and when I'd return. Some wanted to know if I'd be going to Vietnam. I told them that it was very unlikely I'd end up in Vietnam, and that I'd most likely end up attending drills one weekend a month and serving two weeks of active duty per year.

Tuesday, July 4th, 1972, was a day that would remain etched my memory for many years to come. It started out like any other Independence Day celebration. I attended the local parade and helped out with the family BBQ. When evening arrived, I went with friends to the local swimming pool association down the street from my home, where we had a perfect view of the park located a few blocks to the east and, more importantly, the town's annual fireworks display.

We sat in an open convertible listening to music and chatting idly while waiting for the fireworks display scheduled to begin at 9:30. At 9:15, the pyrotechnics team launched a large aerial bomb. The loud report signaled 15 minutes until show time.

The crowd of several thousand spectators closed in on stage center, a roped-off area about the size of two football fields. As show time approached, some of the spectators lit sparklers and small firecrackers. Every once in a while, someone would throw a cherry bomb into the middle of the open space that separated the crowd from stage center. The smell of punk smoke permeated the air. At 9:30, a second large aerial bomb was launched. It was show time!

From my vantage point at the swimming pool several blocks away, I watched the show unfold. Each mortar round left its launch tube with a muffled "thump," leaving a trail of red-hot embers in its wake as it climbed skyward. One by one, the pyro team thrilled the crowd with sky-high explosions full of color and smoke.

About ten minutes into the show, one of the rounds prematurely exploded as it cleared the launch tube. Burning embers from the payload found their way into a nearby stack of rounds waiting to be launched. Several of the rounds exploded at once, setting off a chain reaction. The result was a most spectacular display, the likes of which I had never seen.

We waited for more. After ten minutes, we noticed people leaving the area on foot and in automobiles. We figured the show must be over and wondered why. The fireworks shows usually lasted an hour. This particular show ended in less than ten minutes.

The next day, I learned what happened from people who were at stage center. A friend described it as a war zone. Flaming rounds shout out horizontally from the launch area in all directions. Rounds exploded just feet above the crowd. People close to stage center flattened themselves to the ground, covering their heads. Parents shielded children by lying on top of them. A few nearby homes caught fire and the flames were extinguished. One person died of a heart attack in the rush to get away.

The Brookfield Village Council met later that month and, after much debate, voted to abolish the annual Independence Day fireworks celebration. Thus ended a tradition that dated back to several years before I was born.

Lackland

The day of my departure arrived. That morning, I traveled to the airport with my dad and brother, Martin. Older than me by seventeen months, he had started his military service the previous year, electing to become an aircraft crew chief. Martin would accompany me on my journey to Texas, while dad stayed behind and caught up on some paper work in his office at O'Hare.

On board the airplane, a Boeing C-97, the passengers included me, the crew chief, my brother, the assistant crew chief and one other recruit. The plane made stops in Springfield, Illinois, and Birmingham, Alabama, to pick up additional recruits. By the time we landed at Kelly Air Force Base in San Antonio, Texas, we were some 20 strong.

The airplane taxied to a parking spot on the ramp at Kelly. The pilots kept one engine running to provide electrical and hydraulic power. The crew chief opened the passenger door at the rear of the aircraft and lowered the passenger steps. A blast of hot, humid Texas air hit me in the face. I looked down the steps to see an Air Force training instructor (TI) waiting to greet us. I looked at my brother and shook his hand goodbye. Then I followed my fellow recruits down the steps.

The TI's face was young and stern. He wore no smile and his eyes were hidden from view by a pair of gold frame, military-issue sunglasses. I imagined his eyes full of anger and disdain as he directed us to form two ranks of ten men and walk in this formation toward and through the doors of the military passenger terminal.

As we passed behind the aircraft wing, the pilot mistakenly unfeathered the propeller of the single running engine. This caused a sudden gust of wind that lifted the TI's trooper hat off his head and sent it skipping down the ramp. The TI muttered an obscenity while he scurried after his hat. I looked toward the nose of the aircraft and saw the pilot waving his hand out of the cockpit window. It was as if he was saying, "Sorry Sergeant! My fault!" Perhaps he said something else.

We carried our bags through the passenger terminal toward a set of double doors that led to the parking lot. Outside was an Air Force blue school bus. The TI told us to stack our bags at the rear of the bus and take a seat toward the front. Ten minutes later we arrived at our home away from home: Lackland Air Force Base, "Gateway to the Air Force."

We stepped off the bus and joined 30 other recruits who had arrived earlier that day. All were future Guardsmen. There were four additional TIs to greet us. All of the TIs, save for one, were dressed in short-sleeved tan shirts and matching trousers. The other TI was dressed in a light blue shirt with dark blue trousers. All of their uniforms were pressed and creased to perfection. The shine on their shoes was dazzling. Each wore trooper hats and gold frame, military-issue sunglasses.

One of the TIs directed us to form five ranks of ten recruits. Centered on the sleeves of his uniform was his insignia of rank, a patch consisting of a white star inside a dark blue circle. Extending like wings from the dark blue circle were three white stripes. Below the dark blue circle were two additional stripes. Five stripes identified this TI as a Technical Sergeant (TSgt.). Above the right pocket of his shirt was a dark blue rectangular tag with white letters bearing the name "Bradley." He was joined by a TI of the same rank, whose name above his shirt pocket read "Rennie."

There we stood, 50 recruits in total, all of us from different towns and different backgrounds, and all wearing different styles and colors of clothes. What a contrast to these men dressed to military precision in their uniforms. Because of the various colors recruits wore upon their arrival, they were jokingly referred to as rainbows. There was a marching song created in the rainbows' honor.

"Rainbow, Rainbow don't be blue. Your TI was a rainbow too."

TSgt. Bradley directed us to face him and stand at attention. Our response was not automatic. What ensued was 50 young men positioning themselves. Some quickly became rigid with feet together and hands at their sides while others took their time positioning themselves. This prompted TSgt. Bradley to bark at us in his loudest command voice, "I said, ATTENTION!"

One or two individuals somehow found humor in TSgt. Bradley's frustration and smirked. Their behavior did not go unnoticed. TSgt. Rennie approached one smirking recruit and asked him in a low but angry voice, "Did TSgt. Bradley say something funny?"

"No," was the recruit's response.

"No SIR!" shouted TSgt. Rennie directly into the ear of now-unsmirking recruit.

"NO SIR!" the recruit responded.

Because of our ineptitude, we practiced the art of coming to attention for the next 10 minutes. I recall one TI walking in between our ranks as we rehearsed. He was the coolest looking, most handsome and clean-cut TI of them all. As he passed by, I could smell his aftershave.

It was a fresh, citrusy mix that offered relief from the hot, humid Texas air that afternoon. The scent stuck in my nostrils and embedded itself in my memory. I received a bottle of it for Christmas that same year. It's Eau Savauge by Christian Dior, and I still wear it to this day.

After our impromptu drill practice, TSgt. Bradley stood before us and introduced himself and the other TIs. There was Master Sergeant Gingrich, Training Superintendent and TSgt. Rennie, Training Assistant to TSgt. Bradley. Then there was Staff Sergeant Smith, the guy who met us at the airplane. Finally, there was Staff Sergeant Ellis. Bradley told us that Smith and Ellis were classroom instructors and TIs in training. One day Smith and Ellis would form a military instruction team like Bradley and Rennie. The TIs took up positions on either side of MSgt. Gingrich, who then stepped forward.

Gingrich addressed us with a sharp tone. "Men. On behalf of the Commander of the 37th Training Wing and the Commander of the 3726th Training Squadron, I want to welcome you to Lackland Air Force Base. Over the next six weeks, you will undergo a transformation from civilian to airman. It is the job of the men on my right and left to see that this is done. If you do not allow these men to perform their job, or if you become deficient in the performance of your own job, you will meet with me. I can assure you that is a meeting you will find to be most unpleasant. Do your job. Study hard. Cooperate and graduate!" Then we were dismissed to the dormitory and told to leave our bags outside for retrieval later.

As we approached the entrance to our two-story World War II-style dormitory, we heard a loud voice directing a small group of five uniformed recruits to "fall in." The recruits, dressed in baggy green fatigues, dropped what they were doing and formed a line in single file. We all stopped to watch.

The TI bellowed an order. "Detail! A-Ten-Hut!" The recruits snapped to attention. Then another order, "Half step – March!" The recruits stepped off smartly with their left feet and marched stomping past the front of our formation. We all thought, "Oh my God. What have we gotten ourselves into?"

We waited as the small detail passed, then one by one we entered our dormitory. We were greeted by two recruits who directed us to our bunks and told us to stand by. Each bunk was made up in military white collar, with the olive green top blanket pulled so tightly that a coin could bounce off of it. Some recruits didn't get the message to "stand by" and lounged on their bunks.

A few minutes later the TI team entered the barracks. Bradley spied one of the recruits lounging on his bunks.

"What the hell do you think it this is, airman? A hotel?"

"No, Sir!"

"Stand at attention when I address you! Are you tired?"

"No, Sir!"

"Do you want to sing a lullaby to your fellow airmen?"

"No, Sir!"

"Would you like it if I sang a lullaby to you, Airman?"

"No, Sir!"

"You don't like my singing?"

"No, Sir! I mean – Yes – I like your singing!"

"This is the way I sing, Airman, and you better like it!"

"Yes, Sir!"

"Now, everybody! Fall out and fall in outside on the double!"

We scrambled outside. The TIs were screaming at us and barking orders along the way. It was hazing and harassment, to be sure. It was also imposed discipline in its purest form.

For the next half hour, we practiced falling in and falling out of the dormitory until we were able to accomplish the task within 60 seconds.

Sweat poured from our faces when the TI team ended the exercise and marched us off to the mess hall for evening chow. Along the way, we heard a bugler in the distance begin playing Retreat.

Bradley called the formation to a halt. Then he told us to remain at attention and place our hands over our hearts. Meanwhile, Bradley positioned himself facing the direction of the bugler and saluted with slow, exact movements. His actions were respectful and demonstrated the type of military drill precision he wanted us to achieve. I will never forget the symbolic figure of duty and pride that TSgt. Bradley imparted on me and my flight members that late Sunday afternoon in Texas.

So began our indoctrination into military life. In the short span of six weeks, we went from a bumbling mass of rainbow-clothed civilians to a well-disciplined flight of 50 recruits.

Our first days were filled with haircuts, clothing issue, uniform wear and care, dormitory upkeep and inspection requirements. Later we had drill practice, weapons training and immunizations. We attended classes on military history and personal finance. Physical training was conducted daily, before breakfast and in the relative cool of the mornings.

During the final week, our flight performed flawlessly during drill competition and achieved some of the highest academic and marksmanship scores ever recorded at Lackland.

We distinguished ourselves and delighted our leadership when it was announced that our flight took all honors on evaluation day. This crowning achievement earned us an extra town pass.

One week after evaluation day we graduated. That evening, we emptied our footlockers, packed our duffel bags and suited up in our blue dress uniforms. We were free to roam around the barracks area while awaiting transportation to our next base of assignment. Bradley and Rennie stopped by. They were dressed in civilian clothes and they spoke to us like human beings. They told us that it's part of their job to instill discipline and how they began to back off once they saw we were disciplining ourselves.

They told us how proud they were of us and hoped that one day we'd drop them a letter to let them know where we ended up and how we were getting along. I'm sad to report that I never did write that letter, I hope this chapter makes up for that oversight.

Keesler

Early the next morning, a Greyhound bus showed up. Everyone bound for Keesler AFB was directed to board. I loaded my duffel bag in the lower compartment and stepped onto the bus. We collected a few other men at another squadron before departing Lackland.

The trip to Keesler AFB lasted ten hours. The route took us through the towns of Houston and Beaumont, Texas; Lake Charles and Baton Rouge, Louisiana; and Gulfport, Mississippi. Keesler is situated two blocks from the Gulf of Mexico within the town of Biloxi, Mississippi.

Before departing from Lackland, we were told that the dormitories at Keesler were modern and air-conditioned, with no more than two men per room. When we arrived early that Saturday evening, we were mustered into an open-bay dorm with no air conditioning. It was late August, and the heat and humidity along the Gulf of Mexico made for an uncomfortable evening.

A staff sergeant who was a member of the team formed to process us upon arrival told us that our dormitory was a temporary lodging facility and that we'd get our permanent dormitory assignments in the next day or so. However, we were also told we could dress in civilian clothes during non-duty hours, and to relax and enjoy our free time. And oh yes, by the way, the Airmen's Club is just down the street! There was a rush to get showered and dressed in our civilian clothes. We looked funny wearing our rainbow uniforms with our short "pinger" hair.

The following Monday I received my permanent dormitory assignment and was trucked to the 3399th Student Squadron in Keesler's "Triangle" student housing area. The three-story barracks buildings were shaped like an "H," constructed of concrete block and painted white. My room was located on the 2nd floor near the center of the "H."

As I entered my room, a guy wearing two stripes on his sleeve looked out at me from a room across the hall and down a few doors. He pointed at me and said that he was my bay chief and he'd be down to see me in a few minutes.

I entered a Spartan room with unmade bunks on opposing walls. Two desks occupied the far wall and storage lockers filled the wall next to the door. The bay chief entered my room less than two minutes later, introduced himself as Ed, and said that he was from Madison, Wisconsin. When I told Ed that I was from the Chicago suburbs, he was glad to hear the news because, as he put it, "The rest of these guys are from outside the Midwest. They don't like the Packers or the Bears!" My roommate turned out to be from Hawaii.

For the next 30 weeks, I studied basic and advanced electronic theory. I learned about diodes, transistors, vacuum tubes and how oscillators, mixers and amplifiers work. The theory was put into practice when we began studying how it was applied to design aviation electronics, or avionics for short.

After class and squadron cleaning detail on Friday, there was plenty of time for sightseeing. Most weekends we stayed local, but on more than a few occasions we motored to New Orleans. The drive to the Crescent City took about 90 minutes.

My visits always started with an obligatory stop in the French Quarter, followed by a shopping tour of my favorite antique dealers. If we stayed the night, we'd visit Café' du Monde in the morning for coffee and French-style beignets. On holiday weekends, I'd visit with my paternal grandmother's family in McComb, Mississippi.

For many reasons I felt an attachment to the Gulf Coast, and New Orleans (NOLA) in particular. My first encounter with the area was during the spring of 1969, when my parents brought the family to NOLA; Biloxi, Mississippi and Mobile, Alabama. It was during that trip when my mom told me her mother was born and raised in NOLA. My maternal grandmother's family history in the area dated back to the 1850s. Small wonder that I felt like I was meeting up with an old friend when I arrived at Keesler for technical training in the summer of 1972. In 2014, I visited NOLA with my wife and toured the neighborhoods where my ancestors once lived and thrived. At the end of our visit, we boarded the City of New Orleans at NOLA's Union Station, where my great-granduncle once patrolled as a police officer.

After I graduated from Keesler Technical Training Center in early April 1973 as an Avionics Communications Specialist, I returned to my Illinois home and reverted to weekend warrior status. I brought with me a love of the South and a boatload of memories. I shall never forget the men and women I met during that phase of my military career. I still keep in touch with Ed, my old bay chief. Alas, the future waited for me and it didn't wait long.

Civilian Soldier

My first Unit Training Assembly (UTA) was scheduled for the weekend following my arrival from Biloxi. On that weekend, I met a man in the avionics shop named Jim, who asked if I was looking for work. When I said yes, he told me that he worked for Motorola and that they were looking for people just like me to staff their new facility in Schaumburg, Illinois.

On Jim's advice I traveled to Schaumburg the following Monday and completed a job application. Motorola also administered a test to gauge my knowledge of basic radio and electronic theory. They must have liked what they saw because they offered me a job.

My first position was transmitter final tester on the Mocomm 70 FM 2-way mobile radio. Over the next twelve months, I earned two promotions and made a whopping $4.50 per hour. I loved the work and the people at Motorola, but by mid-1974 the price of gasoline had nearly tripled from the previous year, and my commuting costs took 10% of my net pay. I needed to find a job closer to home. In May, I was hired as a locomotive electrician at General Motors Electro-Motive Division located near McCook. I also started attending classes at College of DuPage in Glen Ellyn.

The next eight years contained many different twists and turns. I saw my mother pass away, got married, became a father and subsequently divorced. All the while I remained faithful to the Illinois Air National Guard. The summer of 1975 marked my fourth year with the Illinois ANG. During Sunday morning of the June UTA weekend, Bill, my avionics supervisor, was surprised to hear that I'd never flown on an air-to-air refueling mission. That afternoon, I found myself taxiing inside a Boeing KC-97L.

My aircraft was the second in a two-ship tanker cell formation. We were scheduled to rendezvous with two F-4C Phantoms from the 183rd TAC Fighter Group located at Capital Airport in Springfield. The rendezvous point was inside a military operating area (MOA) located in the skies over central Illinois known to aviators as the Howard MOA.

We took off from O'Hare at 1:00 p.m. and followed the lead aircraft as it headed southwest and climbed to an altitude of 22,000 feet. After level off, I walked into the spacious cockpit of the KC-97 and seated myself on the edge of the navigator's table just behind the pilot. I peered through the cockpit window and spied the lead ship 1,000 feet below us and one mile off our nose.

We entered the Howard MOA and soon the pilot of the lead tanker banked his aircraft in a left turn to start an orbit while we waited for the receiver aircraft to join us. Our pilot followed the lead aircraft around the orbit, maintaining 1,000 feet vertical separation and staying one mile in trail. When the receivers arrived, the navigator handed me his spare headset and motioned me toward the rear of the airplane so I could view and listen to the air refueling as it unfolded.

What I witnessed can only be described as a marvel of modern aviation. The art of flying two aircraft in close proximity to each other for the purpose of transferring fuel is beautiful yet dangerous. It was thrilling to watch and all I wanted to do from that moment on was to fly.

One bright Saturday morning during late spring of 1980, I was a bleary-eyed 25-year-old standing in formation at the start of another UTA weekend. I listened as Elmer, the flight chief, ran through the roll call. He was prone to mispronouncing names, some by accident; others intentionally.

I was now a Technical Sergeant and almost two years into my first reenlistment. After roll call, Elmer announced that the 108th Air Refueling Squadron was seeking Pilot and Navigator candidates.

I listened as Elmer read through the remainder of the announcements and thought to myself: Tyree. You can stand in this formation each weekend for the remainder of your career or you can do something different – like fly. I applied for a navigator position that day, and 14 months later was informed that I'd been accepted into the program.

Like when I received the phone call in June 1972, I heard opportunity knocking and opened the door, this time into the world of military aviation. I had dreamed of doing something like this from the age of four. There was no turning back. Dad's prophecy was about to unfold.

Officer School to Desert Shield

January 1982 started with a New Year surprise. Although I was informed by letter the previous month that my class date for officer training was scheduled for March, on January 5th I received a phone call from Rudy, the Non-Commissioned Officer in Charge of the base personnel office at O'Hare. Rudy explained that there'd been some sort of regulation change and I had to enter undergraduate navigator training by the time I was 27 years and six months, which was April 16th, 1982.

When Rudy explained that if I entered officer training in March, I would not be commissioned until after the age deadline, I asked if this meant the deal was off. He sort of chuckled and said no and that I'd be entering officer training later in January. He asked me if that was OK and I said it was.

Things really started happening fast. With the help of friends and family, I somehow managed to complete a mountain of paperwork and other arrangements in preparation for my now-imminent departure. On January 25th, I was seated in class at the ANG Academy of Military Science (AMS) located at the I.G. Brown Professional Military Education Center at McGhee Tyson Airport in Knoxville, Tennessee.

The process of turning civilians and civilian soldiers into ANG officers fell on the shoulders of a Major Hugh Large and his instructor staff. Hugh was large as his name implied. Shaking his hand was tantamount to shaking hands with a bear – a large bear. Hugh's mannerisms were laced with Southern pride and professionalism. He was a huge Tennessee Volunteers fan and this fact, along with his size and stature, endeared him to us as Major "Huge" Large.

At AMS, Hugh and his staff managed to accomplish in six weeks what took the regular Air Force 12 weeks: preparing men and women to become officers in the United States Air Force.

During the six weeks of AMS, I roomed with a gentleman named Michael who hailed from a small town in Louisiana and was destined to become an F4 pilot with the Louisiana ANG. Unlike me, Michael and several other classmates had no prior military service. In the first weeks I found myself answering questions and helping the "non-priors" a lot.

Hugh made it a point to explain that prior military service before entering AMS might give some candidates an edge initially, but that history showed that edge became less of a factor towards the end of the six-week AMS curriculum. Hugh was right. Number one in our class was a person with no prior military service.

When I graduated AMS in March 1982 with a commission as a Second Lieutenant, Hugh and his entire staff at AMS had prepared us – not just trained us – for a lifetime of service. Later that month, I started Undergraduate Navigator Training at Mather AFB in Sacramento, California.

During the first few weeks of navigator training, we studied the concept of Airmanship: the acquisition of cockpit skills, sound judgment, situational awareness and positive attitude. We were scheduled for three introductory flights during this segment. These flights were conducted with an Air Force instructor pilot who helped introduce us to the real aviation environment. We performed planning, preflight and inflight tasks as crew members. One such flight allowed us to demonstrate proficiency in aircraft unusual attitude recovery. During this phase I was able to fulfill the promise I had made to myself and my dad when I was four. I flew the T-37 Tweet!

After we completed the Airmanship phase of training we would not fly in the Tweet again until close to graduation day. In between, we flew in the T-43, a converted Boeing 737 with navigation stations for twelve students. Inside the T-43 we honed our skills at dead reckoning, radar, and celestial and low-level navigation. My dad and brother attended the graduation ceremony. Dad proudly pinned a pair of silver wings to my chest and smiled as he patted them into place. He was passing the aviation baton to me.

After Undergraduate Navigator Training, my class split up. Fighter guys went on to tactical navigation and bomber and tanker/transport guys went on to study advanced air navigation techniques such as pressure pattern navigation and aircraft range control. By the end of September 1982, my six months of training at Mather AFB was complete.

The next six months consisted of training in land and sea survival and KC-135. By April 1983, I was home in Illinois and ready to fly as a navigator with the 126th Air Refueling Wing at O'Hare International Airport in Chicago.

Over the course of the next eight years, I completed my college education, a commitment I made to the ANG and a requirement if I was to maintain my status as a commissioned officer. I married for a second time, bought a home, and settled down with my wife in Downers Grove IL, all while serving as a civilian soldier.

My duties as a navigator found me traveling to every corner of the world and many points in between. When Saddam Hussein invaded Kuwait in August 1990, the 126th AREFW was one of the first units to respond to the Headquarters USAF request for tanker support.

The 126th AREFW was tasked with anchoring the eastern end of the Atlantic air bridge. Flying from their base in southern Spain, the KC-135 crews provided round-the-clock air refueling support for aircraft flying into the Middle East. They would rendezvous with receiver aircraft near the Straits of Gibraltar and fly the length of the Mediterranean Sea, handing them off to tanker crews flying out of Egypt. In this way, aircraft could fly nonstop from their bases in the USA to their destinations in the Middle East without having to land. Round-the-clock air refueling was a prime example of the USAF's ability to project its power globally.

During December 1990, the 126th AREFW was relieved of its mission in Spain and ordered to an air base in southwest Saudi Arabia. From there the wing was divided in two. One half deployed to an air base in the United Arab Emirates (UAE) while the other half remained at the base in southwest Saudi Arabia.

I deployed with my crew to the UAE while my brother remained in Saudi Arabia. I would see him once more on the day before the shooting war started and not again until after the ceasefire.

Desert Storm and Epilogue

We arrived at Al Dhafra air base near Abu Dhabi, UAE, on Thursday, January 10th, 1991. Members of the 363rd TAC Fighter Wing from Shaw AFB, South Carolina greeted us as our host tenant. We were relative newcomers to the base, as the 363rd had been on site since August 9th the previous year.

As it turned out, although the 363rd had more than enough room to house the members of our unit in its massive tent city, it could not accommodate our aircraft. There just was not enough room on the parking ramp – it was full of F-16s. The master plan called for 12 KC-135 aircraft (six from the 126th AREFW, Illinois ANG and six from the 121st AREFW, Ohio ANG) to be parked at Abu Dhabi IAP.

The airport was located 20 minutes down the road by car. The aircraft and deployed members from Illinois and Ohio formed the 1712th Expeditionary Air Refueling Wing – Provisional. Our base operations building was no bigger than a large shack and was located in the general aviation area of the airport. The building was previously used by the USSR, which had abandoned its mission and the building sometime during the mid-1980s.

At Al Dhafra, the 363rd Civil Engineers were notified of our forward deployment about two weeks in advance. They erected forty new tents and equipped them with cots, sheets and blankets. They also erected four new shower houses and added a wing to the base dining facility. Everything was operational and waiting for us upon our arrival. Now, that's planning!

My crew was housed in a tent on the perimeter of the tent city about 500 yards from the runway. All was quiet that evening but at 6:00 the next morning, eight F-16s armed to the teeth took to the sky in pairs. They were anything but quiet as the pilots used full afterburner during their takeoff roll. The morning serenade continued for a few more days and then stopped without explanation. There were no F-16 flights on the morning of January 16th, 1991.

The Mother of All Battles started the next morning at 2:10, Baghdad time. I was trying to sleep. My crew and I had flown a round-trip cargo run between UAE and Saudi the previous day. When we returned during the late evening, our squadron commander ordered us directly into crew rest. We looked at our CO, who didn't say a word. He didn't have to. We all knew the shooting war was about to start.

We were directed to a makeshift bunk area located next to the operations area. We napped for about an hour. By midnight the operations area was alive with activity. Air crews involved with the first wave were arriving and going through the motions of planning and briefing their refueling assignments.

I heard their muffled voices through the thin wall separating us. The men on the other side of the wall were talking, joking, laughing. They were busy completing the many small but essential tasks required before they could haul 200,000 pounds of jet fuel into the air.

I wanted to be part of the first wave. I wanted to be in that room and see their faces. They were my friends. They were men whom I'd come to know and respect. They were going to war and some of them may not come back.

I must have dozed off because the next thing I knew the noise coming from the other side of the wall was replaced by the whine of jet engines on the parking ramp. I got out of my bunk and wandered outside.

The air was cool and dry. It was perfect flying weather for heavy jets. Rounding the corner of the operations shack, I saw the silhouettes of several KC-135s lined up on the taxiway.

Moments later, the first aircraft taxied onto the runway and began its takeoff roll. It was followed 60 seconds later by the next aircraft and the next, until all were airborne. They used no lights on departure, and soon all I could hear was the fading rumble of jet exhaust as the aircraft climbed toward their refueling areas somewhere high over the Persian Gulf.

I walked inside the crew rest area and climbed back in my bunk.

I thought of my wife, wondering if and when I'd see her again.

I heard low muffled voices through the wall before I drifted off to sleep.

When I woke up sunlight was streaming through the windows. I heard Jerry, our pilot and crew leader, speaking in a low voice with a guy about our crew's report time. When the guy left, Jerry announced that we had to report to the briefing area in 15 minutes. I got up and silently donned my flight suit and boots. The rest of the crew did the same. It was 7:30.

We strolled into the briefing area, where a fresh pot of coffee was brewing. The operations staff had been on duty since 4:00 p.m. the previous day. Crews from the first wave were beginning to return and go through debrief. We would fly one of the returning aircraft once it was refueled. Meanwhile, we busied ourselves with mission planning activities just like the crews had the prior evening.

All the information we required for our sortie was contained in the Air Tasking Order (ATO). The ATO provided our takeoff time, fuel load, refueling track, rendezvous and refueling control times and altitudes, type of receiver aircraft and estimated fuel requirements. The ATO also contained the modes, codes and call signs of every sortie for that day, including our own.

Our Intel officer gave us a situation report that included a triple A and surface-to-air threat update. It was too early to tell, but from the looks of things one could believe the good guys were already winning.

We launched on our first of 42 combat support sorties at 10:00 a.m., on January 17th, 1991. We flew a northwest heading from our base in the UAE and entered an orbit 25,000 feet directly over the U.S.S. Theodore Roosevelt. We spent two hours on station and refueled numerous U.S. Navy fighter aircraft before finally declaring "bingo fuel." We were cleared off station by "Red Crown," the rough equivalent of air traffic control for the Navy, and landed back at our base an hour later at 2:00 p.m.

So began a daily rhythm of 12 hours on and 12 hours off. The off time started as soon as we departed the operations area. We'd spend an hour in debrief and depart at 3:00 p.m. Our next duty window started at 3:00 a.m. the following morning and would last until 3:00 p.m. that afternoon. We could be scheduled to fly anytime within the 12-hour window. Everything depended on the ATO, which could change multiple times in a day.

One day after we returned from an early sortie, I walked out to the general aviation ramp at Abu Dhabi IAP to enjoy the warm desert morning. The sky was clear except for darkness noticeable on the horizon in all directions. I asked the wing intelligence officer about the dark horizon. He replied it was smoke from burning oil wells in Iraq and Kuwait. And we're breathing this stuff, I said to myself.

Then we heard the unmistakable rumble of a Harley-Davidson motorcycle. We looked out across the empty general aviation ramp and saw an Arab dressed in full white robe and headdress riding a Sportster across the huge expanse of concrete. It was the damndest thing. Later I found out the motorcycle belonged to Al Masaood and Sons Harley-Davidson dealership. I have a t-shirt from the dealer. It's a beautiful thing.

By the end of February 1991, Kuwait was liberated, the Iraqi forces were in a shambles and a ceasefire was declared. The coalition forces achieved their strategic objectives. Soon we would be able to travel home. Soon, but not soon enough. My unit was tasked with supporting a newly established no-fly zone situated over the entire country of Iraq. For the next week, we waited for orders that would enable us to return home. In the meantime, our crew duty days were relaxed to eight hours on and 16 hours off.

Three days before we departed for home, the elements of the 126th AREFW left behind in Saudi Arabia arrived in Abu Dhabi. I was reunited with my brother and our entire wing was reconstituted. My brother and I celebrated that evening along with many other wing members.

We flew home in the first group of three KC-135s and arrived with much fanfare on March 12th, 1991, at O'Hare IAP, where our spouses, parents and children greeted us. I was treated to a free breakfast at a local restaurant before returning to our home in Downers Grove.

In December 1991, my wife and I became the proud parents of a baby boy. Today, our son is a Tennessee Volunteer. He graduated from the University of Tennessee, Knoxville in May 2015.

In the middle of the campus at that great university, at the entrance to Circle Park, is the statue of the Torch Bearer. In his right hand he holds an eternal flame high in the air for all to see. The flame from the torch guides the way toward enlightenment. He wears a sword for security and in his left hand holds a globe of Winged Victory.

I know now why we put our asses on the line during that stormy evening in March 1991. It was about securing freedom and the knowledge that everyone should be able to live life free from the tyranny of dictators and autocrats. We put it out there for our children and their children. As citizen soldiers, we volunteered to train and fight, if need be, for the future generations of Americans who will follow. It was always for them, as well it should be. They are the ones who will keep America free long after these words are forgotten.

TSgt Bradley and TSgt Rennie: God Bless You wherever you are. ✧

Pat Tyree was born in 1954. He is the fourth of five children born to Hal C. and Mary T. Tyree. He grew up in Brookfield, Illinois and attended St. Barbara's Catholic Grade School and Lyons Township HS. Pat has shared a love of flying since he was four years old.

Pat entered service with Illinois Air National Guard on July 5, 1972. His mom had to sign his enlistment papers because he was a minor.

He attended Basic Military Training at Lackland AFB, San Antonio, TX from July – August, 1972. After BMTS, Pat transferred to Keesler AFB, Biloxi, MS, where he trained to become and avionics repair specialist. Pat returned from his training in April of 1973 and continued life as a citizen soldier with the 125th AREFW located at Chicago's O'Hare International Airport. While enlisted, Pat worked on Boeing KC-97L and KC-135 aircraft and attained the rank of E5 (Technical Sergeant).

In January of 1982, Pat entered officer training at the ANG Academy of Military Science, located at McGhee Tyson Airport, Knoxville, Tennessee. He was commissioned as a 2nd Lieutenant on March 4, 1982 and completed undergraduate navigator training in August of 1982.

He served as a navigator on KC-135 aircraft for 15 years.

It was during this time in Pat's career that he and his colleagues were called on to support Operations Desert Shield and Desert Storm between August 1990 and March 1991. Pat retired from the Illinois Air National Guard on July

4, 1997 with the rank of LtCol. He received an Air Medal for his efforts during the first Desert War.

In civilian life, Pat worked as project engineer at General Motors and as a Program Manager for Motorola. Pat is currently retired and pursuing his private pilot certification. Pat is married to Julie Marie Schaefer. They have two children and one grandson. ✦

wptyree@sbcglobal.net

Mike Wohead

COMPANY A, 818TH ENGINEERS AVIATION BATTALION: 1X ENGINEER COMMAND

Aviation Engineers In Mobile Warfare

This is a brief consolidation of stories and interesting happenings during our stay in the States, England, and my duties in France, Belgium, and Germany. This compilation of stories tells about what so many paid the ultimate price for.

It is intended to compliment the men in our responsibility and to give credit to the officers I had the privilege to serve under, and due respect to the enlisted men we were responsible for.

It is interesting to note that there were no professional football players or Olympic wrestlers on the front lines; most of the combat was by the "little guys."

Great glory and honor has been paid the men who fought and died in the Air Corps, but without the Aviation Engineers and the hasty airfields, they would not be able to fly. The Aviation Engineers were U.S. Army assigned to the Air Corps. So we were assigned many locations for runways that were for the benefit of the Air Corps without Army approval.

SERVICE IN THE U.S. ARMY: 1941 to 1945

I was drafted on 21 October 1941, and it was a typical October day: cloudy and rather cool. Our reporting area was the CB&O railroad station in Downers Grove, Illinois.

My dad and mom took me to the station, and there were about 25-30 other draftees present. It was a rather quiet group and I knew only one person there — Eddy Reifschneider — and it was the last time I saw him. We were transferred to different units and parts of the country.

It was a slow trip to Chicago and from that moment, everything became sort of hazy. We went through medical examination, and were issued Army clothing, listened to a couple of talks and the spent the night in Chicago. The next day, after a few lectures, we had a timed test. To me, at the start, it was just a test. But I tried to answer the questions as fast as possible, and then came back to answer the ones I passed over the first time through. I never realized after scoring 138 points, how important this test would be for the rest of my Army career. The last day in Chicago went by slowly, and then we were put on a train and went to Camp Grant in Rockford, Illinois.

Here was our introduction to close order drill, additional medical tests, and also to KP (Kitchen Police, or peeling potatoes) and mopping the floor in the mess hall.

The stay in Rockford was only a couple of weeks, and one weekend, I had a pass to go home. The Sergeant took me to a filling station in Lombard on North Avenue, and I walked home on Fairview Avenue through Downers Grove. Strange as it may sound, the walk was about 7 to 8 miles, and not a single car passed me going either direction.

It was a sad weekend, and my father took me back to the filling station on Sunday for my return to Camp Grant.

Time passed slowly, but within a couple of days, they started sending soldiers to various training camps. In a couple of days, I was sent by train to Fort Leonard Wood, Missouri. Here we went into more advanced training, from close order drill, to hikes, the rifle and slowly into the many angles of Army work.

Our Sergeant was Sullivan, and although we were all recruits, he let us know quickly that we were in the Army now.

We were allowed weekend passes to the nearby cities of Rolla, Newburg, and Waynesville.

After a rather quiet week, on Sunday morning, 7 December, the news came over the air and everyone stopped and listened to it. The Japanese had bombed Pearl Harbor in Hawaii, and the news was continuous all day long.

We were stationed in huts at that time, and everyone went outside to discuss the matter further. Sergeant Sullivan couldn't add any further information to what we'd heard. On Monday, President Roosevelt, before a packed Senate, read the verdict that the United States had declared war on Japan, Germany, and their allies.

The easy calm of the training camp changed immediately. No longer did we take rifle training or machine gunning as a pastime — training became intense, and everyone realized that there were serious days coming.

This was evident on New Year's Day. It seemed that everyone went home for a weekend pass or even for a couple of hours. I arrived at the St. Louis station at about 11 AM, figuring I had plenty of time to get back to camp. It didn't take long for the entire station to become full, and the only way you could get through the doors to the train was to twist yourself through as the doors opened.

Eventually they took all the passenger cars they could find, and engines to make a train, and finally at 11 PM, I got on a train. I spent the night sleeping on the floor of the ladies' restroom. We arrived at Ft. Leonard Wood at 4 AM.

Training continued, but very slowly. Two or three soldiers were called daily, and sent to their assignment organizations. By the end of January, my turn finally came, and I was sent to Camp Murray, Washington, a camp associated with McChord Field. This was – and is – the most northwest defense of this country. Here I was assigned to the 813th Engineer Aviation Company, with Captain Dent L. Lay as commander, and First Sergeant Grubbs.

Things immediately changed from the easier-going at Ft. Leonard Wood. Basic training turned serious, as did the rifle range and machine gun training. We also began working on the construction of runways and airfield maintenance.

I progressed from Private to Acting Sergeant in a short while, and on 25 February 1942, received an order to report to McChord Field to supervise slit trenching for the protection of McChord Field personnel in the event of a Japanese bombing.

The trenches were zigzagged, so that a person could shift from one side to the other in the event of airplane strafing. The trenches were 6 feet deep and about 20 feet in length.

We completed the trenches, as we had a company of 170 men to do the labor. Daily radio messages at that time were of potential air bombing, and the war in the Pacific continually increased.

Shortly after this venture, I was appointed First Sergeant in only four and one-half months. Everything was moving fast at this time, and one of the luckiest things that happened to me was that I was transferred out of the 813 Battalion to the 833rd as a new cadre. The 813 were sent to the islands of Attu and Kiska on the Aleutian Islands in Alaska. This was one of the most dangerous places to be assigned, weather-wise due to the bitter cold.

Prior to leaving, Captain Lay said, "Sergeant, I am leaving a couple of men that would only be trouble for us, and we won't be able to replace them, but you can." A couple of days before they left, Sergeant Grubbs said, "Sergeant, I will give you one piece of advice: "If you ever get a friend in the company who works for you, tear off your stripes, because if you don't, he will tear them off of you." This advice I followed during my two years as a First Sergeant.

During the last days in the 813th Engineer Aviation Battalion, time was urgent and went very fast. The preparation of the company to leave, more intensive review of the conditions we were training under, and finally they left and I was left with a cadre of a few men, and a couple of the men Capt. Lay did not want in his company.

My entire stay in McChord Field was in four-man tents, with a small cone-shaped wood burning heater to keep the humidity and chill out of the room. The day the 813th Engineers left, we were moved from the Camp Murray section to McChord Field, and our tents were on the south side of the end of the runway. So planes were constantly taking off and landing just nearby.

One day, while doing close order drills between our company and the airfield, as B-25 2-engine plane took off, the right engine gave out, forcing power into the left motor. The plane veered to the right, crashed, and exploded. If it had been the left engine that'd failed, and the plane had veered to the left, my entire company would have been wiped out.

Life at McChord Field consisted of getting new recruits daily, doing close-order drills and various other Army training maneuvers. We were C Company — the other companies were getting a full complement of officers, while my company did not have any officers.

Eventually, Captain Emil Bauer was assigned to our company, and Sgt. Grubbs' advice was put to good use quickly. Secrecy was always stressed, and perhaps it was at its highest level at that point. For instance, Major Beeler, our battalion commander, lived on the post with his wife. The way she found out that we were leaving is that she saw him get on the train.

THE PACIFIC THEATER

The Japanese Air Force bombed Pearl Harbor on 7 December 1941, and at that time, I was stationed at Ft. Leonard Wood, Missouri. After that date, from being in the Army on a casual basis, everything changed to a very serious training program and intense U.S. Army approach to things. I helped to supervise digging slit trenches at McChord Field in Washington, and also at that time, the United States moved all of the Japanese people living on the west coast. This was unfortunate to many U.S. citizens, but after Pearl Harbor, who could you trust?

The 833rd Engineers Aviation Battalion was activated in April 1942, and after intensive training and forming of the company, we finally left for Fort Dix New Jersey in August 1942.

Getting ready to leave McChord Field became a busy time, as the men had to be checked medically, and also, all of us were informed regarding creating of our wills, and other necessary papers. Most of all, we were kept on guard, and continually reminded the men of secrecy and other data. There were no memos or diaries to be made. This is why so many dates are omitted as they would only be some date remembered by the individuals. We were finally placed on the train, and started the long journey to New Jersey.

Meals on the train were two per day, and the confinement to the aisle between seats made the journey rather burdensome for the cooks and other personnel.

Secrecy during the travel was rather difficult for some soldiers. The train had to stop in cities along the way for water and other supplies. In some cases, some of the soldiers from Montana saw their parents at a stop, and ran to them. They were court-martialed later, but given a light sentence.

The stay in Fort Dix, NJ, was a matter of wait-and-see. We had nothing scheduled in the way of close order drill or anything else, it was monotonous, and keeping the men engaged was a problem for the company commander, Captain Bauer. Drinking was everywhere, and one day we made a tour of the barracks and found a number of open and full bottles of whiskey.

When we finally arrived in New York Harbor it took several days to board all the troops for our ship. We were ushered into the hold of the luxury ship from Argentina, the USS Uruguay. When we got to our quarters, which consisted of four deck cots, we realized it was just an Army troop ship. We departed for Halifax, Nova Scotia

The convoy consisted of 26 ships and two sub-chasers. We went close to Iceland, because the waves made it hard for the submarine to get a good shot, and zigzagged every six minutes to keep from being in a straight line. Our sub-chasers dropped charges two times during the trip.

We were fed twice a day, and because of the rampant seasickness, we spent one day in the hold, which was four sections down, and then at noon every day, we went on deck. It was cold, but at least you were not seasick.

We were at sea fourteen days. We arrived at Hadleigh, England, in August 1942. Here we started constructing concrete runways and airfield and other facilities building. Because we were faced with the coming winter in England, we made Quonset huts for the troops. When completed, it would be the first time we lived in huts instead of tents for almost a year.

German planes made sure that we knew they were around, as almost every night, one would fly overhead. It was routine for a German plane to fly over the area and drop a bomb at night and return to Germany. They were called Bed-Check Charlies, and I felt the wind of many bombs. Daily, we could see British planes go on their missions and return. They spent most of the time in night raids, except for the Spitfires, which flew in daytime.

We quickly became established as a construction company. Working time was the total daylight hours, and so work was done under lights. It almost became routine for a time.

Once a week, the Shower Truck would show up. This consisted of placing a plastic fence in a square in the middle of a field, and a showerhead in the middle. On a very cool day, it was an interesting pastime to shed clothes for a shower, and see how quickly you could get your clothes back on again for warmth.

We were also allowed one pass per week, and most of the day passes were to London. We would go by truck to Colchester and then by train to London. It was always a good time unless you accidently got to London when there was an air-raid by the German Luftwaffe. I was caught in some of these and found the underground train or streetcar stations were very comfortable. They would always be filled with women and children.

The Covent Garden Ballroom was always an easy place to go to for an evening. There were always a lot of British girls there, and it was a grand ballroom: a center bandstand, and when orchestras changed places, both bands would play the same melody, and when the stand made a half-turn, the new orchestra took over. Gone With The Wind played weekly in local movie theatres. In many cases, when a person went to London, he would also visit Piccadilly Circus at night.

On many of my trips to London, I would go to Bedfordshire, where my brother, John, was stationed. He was in Ordnance and in turn was on one of the first U.S. Bombardier flights over Germany – the 306th Bombardier group. He loaded fragmentation bombs and heavier bombs for mass destruction.

It was interesting to watch a squadron of planes take off in the morning. They would line up, almost motor to tail, and get on the runway as soon as possible so they could fly in formation, save gas, and leave for the mission. To hear the noise of the engines of 25 planes in the air made a shiver go through your body. And their return was something else. The duties of the airfield continued until the last plane returned. As the count neared 20 the attitude on the airfield shifted, as everyone slowly counted to 21… 22… and many times up to 23, 24,

25, when everyone made it back. We always saw planes that were shell-shocked: travelling with one missing motor, imbedded shrapnel, or showing other results of having flown over Germany. On one plane I counted twenty bullet holes. In all cases, repairs had to be made within one hour, so the planes could fly again immediately.

I was at the airfield one day when one soldier was going up for this 23rd mission. I can assure you, he was in a very thoughtful mood. Pilots who completed 25 missions were permitted to go home. The 306th Bombardier group flew 343 missions, 9,614 sorties, dropped 22,614 tons of bombs, and lost 171 planes. The Air Force in England lost more men then all of the Army, Navy, and Marines combined in the Pacific.

Traveling at night after 1800h to a new fast-repair airstrip was always interesting. One night, I asked my Jeep driver to look forward and watch out for the cat-eyes of approaching vehicles, as I looked in the air and kept repeating "You're between the trees" which was the only way we knew we remained on the road due to the blackout conditions.

The training at the Officers training school started the first day. We were introduced to Captain Neal, and from that day, we took part in doing and instructing close order drills, taking long marches, studying machine guns, American and British hand guns, taking target practice qualifying with a rifle, mortar shooting, and also the torpedo.

Everything was a constant instruction and serious training. One of the training sessions we had every time the British or higher officials showed up was the crossing of a river and attacking. Because the lake used was shallow, they put all of the shorter men in this presentation. When you came out, you were soaking wet, so we had to go to the barracks, undress outside, and run quickly to our rooms to clean up and put dry clothes on. We always hoped there would be no women around.

Saturday inspection was always seriously considered, and Capt. Neal would dig you faster for dirty fingernails than for any other reason. He said that if you have a dirty rifle, you can be killed for it; if you have dirty fingernails and contaminate the food in the kitchen, you could make the entire company sick (and in turn, useless for combat). I sometimes received letters from my sister and brother via V-Mail. It was so great to receive mail.

The Officer training school in England did not cover any one branch of service. We had candidates from the infantry, Air Corps, tank divisions, engineers.

The reason for this was that the Army did not give commissions to soldiers and leave them with the original company. In this way, you were assigned to another unit, and in this way there was no friendship involved.

There were 12 men from the infantry, and within two weeks after D-Day, six of them were dead.

Upon graduation (my brother, John, attended the ceremony) in October 1943, I was assigned to the 818th Engineer Aviation Battalion, Company A. I immediately went into the finishing and repair of the heavy bomber concrete runways and other maintenance.

Co. A 818 Aviation Engineer Battalion consisted of 170 men and 4 officers. We were the first company in Paris, we were the first and only company to build an airfield in front of the infantry at Luxembourg, and we were the only company at Tulln Airfield in Vienna, Austria.

We were finally stationed about 20 miles from Oxford, England, and at that point the final training began. We did maintenance work and repair in some areas, but it really became the final and detailed instruction for what we were going to do. I was assigned as training coordinator for the entire battalion with Sgt. Arthur McKee as my assistant. Here we received most of the requirements from Col. Hall, who was a very able Battalion Commander. We were scheduled to land at D+2 hrs, but he was promoted to Regiment two weeks before D-Day, and we were changing to D+24 or landing on 30 June.

We landed in 1942 and into late 1943, our airfield was almost complete. It was about this time that Colonel Beeler called me into the battalion HQ and told me that they were submitting my name for Officer Candidate training school. So I went to London to be interviewed by several Colonels and Majors, and finally was released from my duties as a First Sergeant, and went to Officer Training School at Shrivenham Berks, near Oxford.

There were no sad farewells. I went by train to the school. Our first introduction was brief: "You are in an Officer training school. We will try to break you mentally or physically to see if you are Officer material. If not, you will be an officer in the United States Army.

Col. G. Hall was the battalion commander of the 818th Engineer Aviation Battalion, as I transferred out of Officer Training school and was assigned to Co. A under Captain Wiedeman. We repaired and maintained airfields, until we were transferred to serious training to prepare for D-Day landing in France.

CAPTAIN ALBERT F. WIEDEMAN

I had respect and appreciation for all of the company commanders, and battalion commanders under whom I served. However, my respect and admiration for Captain Wiedeman grew, because I was assigned to Co. A of the 818th Engineer Aviation Battalion after graduation from Officer Candidate School. The short service and training for going into the French battle area became more and more advanced as time came closer for the invasion of France.

We landed on Utah Beach in France on June 30, 1944, and followed advancing armies through France to Luxembourg, engaging in the construction of 18 airfields. In the "Bulge" area, the unit was forced to mine and guard our installations. We built 12 south and east strips east of the Rhine. From the day of our landing, his decisions, respect for his men, and operation under difficult conditions increased my respect for him.

We left with a convoy to a new area, he usually gave me the military map and I led the convoy to the new territory. I respected Captain Weideman's confidence, knowledge, respect for his men, and ability to lead, think, and act under trying conditions. I trusted his every decision, even though some were borderline decisions between life and death. I cannot think of anyone I trusted or respected more.

The training was very much combat-oriented, as hiking, gas mask, machine gun, and many other factors to combat were part of the training. For gas mask drill, we usually used a small piece of gas. Eventually, we ran out of these, and Sgt. McKeever and I decided to use a gas grenade instead. When you walk into a room with your gas mask on, it was easy. To test the mask, they'd remove the gas mask and walk outside.

A couple of weeks before D-Day, we were scheduled to land, but Col. Hall was transferred to regiment, and we had Major Cutter for the new Battalion commander, so we were rerouted to D+24: 30 June.

While we were in training for the D-Day departure near Cheltenham, the Nurses Corps sponsored a dance near Oxford, and invited the officers from our outfit and other outfits to attend. I was surprised when two very attractive nurses came to me and said that they would toss a coin and I could guess heads or tails, each of which was assigned to one or the other of them. I couldn't lose, so I spent a very enjoyable evening with a nurse from St. Louis.

We were building a few airfield every couple of weeks. Patton wanted many fields so they could strafe and return in about 25 minutes.

Although we were able to build a hasty airfield in a couple of weeks, we did not have the equipment to sprinkle the runway to keep dust from the takeoff planes from affecting the others. The first few planes went off easily, but the planes had to take off in the blind dust created by the first planes.

To improve takeoff for the planes, we switched to Hessian Strip runways. This was a matter of using a large machine for unrolling the Hessian strip material and impregnating the underside with diesel fuel and then placing it 50/50 over the piece on the ground, and it would seal the piece on the ground.

All of the runways after the first few weeks were built using Hessian Strip, until we built the first airfield in Germany out of pierced plank.

PARIS

The first sign I had of Paris is when I flew over the city after working on an airfield at Versailles.

My first visit to Paris was a rather hasty one. We were to be working on a main airfield north of Paris, but first we had a day to sightsee. When the work was completed, we left in a hurry. This was a concrete airfield and what the Germans did was to excavate holes in different parts of the runway, place bombs and heavy armor shells in the bottom, and then blow them up. So my job was primarily to clean out the holes, pour gravel to fill them, and then pour concrete over the filling. A couple of days, after we had the holes filled, the ordinance came over and said how dangerous it was to lift the bombs and the 105mm shell from artillery guns, under those conditions, after they had dynamite explosions over them.

The odd part of Army life was that when we were leaving France, there was an Officer there from the Aviation Engineers who had a citation for distinct service, and I asked him how he got it. He said, "We had nothing to do, so we kept cleaning the airfield, and our EPT kept sending letters to the Pentagon about it."

Colonel Hall, our battalion commander in training, was killed by a sniper in Paris.

We were building an airfield with a glide angle over St. Lo, France, when 3,500 fighters and bombers bombed the German tanks, thus starting Patton on his way through France. From the airfield, we could see the bombs fall from the planes even without field glasses.

We were building and repairing the airfield, and I flew over Paris, while the German Army was still fighting in the east end.

From here we moved into the Luneville area. When we showed up as a battalion , the Infantry commander told our battalion commander, Col. Cutter, that if he had any jurisdiction over our battalion, he'd be a buck private the next day, for bringing a unit such as ours that close and into combat location.

The P47 Thunderbolt was the fighter plane on most of the airfields we built. Usually, the fields were built for about 60 planes. We were expected to build an airfield in about two weeks. The planes usually started coming in before we were done, and we left for another airfield. We very seldom had much contact with the pilots. We also did not see many returns of the fighter planes, because we were, by then, on a new airfield. General Patton wanted the planes to fly and return in about 15 to 25 minutes so they could fly a new mission.

The right side of every runway was always clear for emergency, or planes in trouble. One day, I had to decide whether to go into the emergency area to the right, or 50 feet to the left, as a plane was crash-landing right where I was working.

There was a day at the Aachen airfield on which I counted 62 planes taking off in 12 minutes, two abreast from each other from each end of the runway, against the wind, heading out to cross the Rhine River.

Church services were always available at any Army camp I was assigned to. The services were always attended by the soldiers. It gave me a chance to see some of the largest and most famous churches in the world.

In London, when we were on a pass, it was always a solace to be able to attend mass in one of the larger churches. When in Paris, I had the opportunity to attend a service at the Notre Dame Cathedral. To this day, I'm amazed at how they built those structures, so many years ago, without the machinery and equipment we used even then.

In some cases, the locations for Catholic mass was given to us as a compass setting, and we'd use a map. I went to the location and, standing alone, felt as if I was in the wrong place. After a short while, another soldier showed up, then a Catholic chaplain showed up, carrying a small case, which turned out to be a small table. He set it up near a stump. Nearing 11:00AM, the Chaplain was preparing to start the mass, and more soldiers slowly came out of the trees as if they were shadows coming into daylight. They were all in full combat dress, and carrying their guns and grenades. The mass was a short one, as the Chaplain had several more places to attend to by the coordinates on the map. The soldiers then slowly disappeared back into the woods; in many cases, they only had a mile or two to the front.

The Chaplain in our battalion spent many hours talking and consoling our men. I was grateful that a Chaplain was assigned to our battalion.

They say there are no atheists in foxholes. If there were, they were probably praying that the ones attending services would be successful.

I had the highest respect for the men of the Army. As a First Sergeant, I found them to be willing, and they had a deep desire to do what was right, and in most cases, agreed with what the Army was trying to do. As an officer, I spent more time with the men in my platoon, and was glad. They had the same determination to get the job done, whatever we had to do. To complete a job so that planes could fly… and they never questioned the conditions they had to work under.

LUNEVILLE, FRANCE

We never knew what airfield we would have to work on next, as the Air Corps would make a suggestion and then we went there to work. This was the condition when our reconnaissance unit arrived at Luneville, to work on the airfield there.

The battalion commander, Col. Cutter, and a small unit would show up and very soon, some of the heavy equipment would start showing up. This was the case at Luneville, and when the infantry commandant saw our unit show up, he told our battalion commander "If I had any control over your unit and you showed up this close to the front to work on an airfield with your equipment, you would be a buck private tomorrow."

The U.S. Tank Corps was still on the west side of Luneville when we were asked to build a hasty airfield on the east side, where we could be easily seen by the enemy. As we worked on the airfield, we heard German armor and ammunition go overhead.

The Germans thought if we built it, they would have an airfield for their jets. Our units thought it would be an airfield for the P47s, P51s, and P38s.

From this airfield we saw the infantry units go into their defense location for the night. We could hear the small arms fire.

One day I was looking down the runway facing east, when I saw a tank about a half-mile north move behind a two-story brick building and fire a couple of rounds of ammunition from the heavy batteries or guns they had. After he fired several rounds, he backed out in just a minute or so, the two-story brick building was blown up by the Germans.

They could have easily placed that load of bombs in the center of our runway any time they wanted to.

We continued to work on the airfield, and it was the first time we lived inside of a building. We could hear shells as they went overhead all night long. How we survived, I do not know.

If I were three feet closer to the machine gun bullets that hit the dirt in front of me, I wouldn't be writing these memoirs. The 50 caliber machine gun bullets came from a sky battle between two German jet fighters and a group of P51s and P47s, because jets could fly over 600 mph, and the maximum speed of the 51s and 47s was around 400 mph. It was no contest, and the jets left.

In the battle area of Luneville, we were near enemy fire at all times. I visited the Emergency tent where medics delivered casualties from the front. Anyone who has watched the TV program M.A.S.H. and thinks that nurses were in tents for TV purposes only is mistaken. I visited the tent many times, I found the nurse working under very rough conditions as well as rough sleeping conditions, too. They would quickly treat a soldier for minor wounds, but a soldier who was seriously wounded would receive intense emergency care, sometimes being placed in an ambulance for shipment to a hospital.

The saddest part of this area was when an Army medical truck was seen coming down the road with a pine branch on top — this was a truck with casualties on board and they had the right of way en route to the burial grounds.

It was from Luneville that one morning that Capt. Wiedeman said that we would leave that day to build an evacuation and hospital field in Luxembourg. So while working on the airfield a couple of days later, an infantry soldier asked me to come and talk to his platoon leader. I met him in a barn as he was looking out the window onto the airfield we were building. He said to me, "That is a beautiful 50-caliber machine gun you have," as he mentioned the rounds per minute and the distance the bullets would reach, and as I agreed with him, he asked, "Do you see that soldier?" as he tipped his chin outward. "That soldier is the Front of the U.S. Army, and you are building an airfield in front of the infantry."

We completed the airfield.

In Luxembourg, we built a supply and evacuation strip in front of the infantry. We repaired roads, and mined bridges, at the edge of the Belgian Bulge, at Esneux, Belgium. We moved into Germany on Christmas Day to build a pierced plank field, at the edge of the Belgian Bulge, at Aachen, Germany.

While in France, there were also many U.S.O. shows, and they were always entertaining. Once, we had no facilities for a large group of people. A show featuring Bing Crosby was scheduled near the front at LeMans, France. When Mr. Crosby found out how close to the front we were, he refused. Bob Hope took his place. He stood on the back of a truck, with very little lights, after sunset, and gave an hour-long program. I doubt if we had even fifty soldiers for the show, but everyone enjoyed it.

We entered Luxembourg on the 15th of September 1944. Between the work on Luxembourg, other repair jobs, and the completion of the Luneville airfield, we spent the time until we left for Belgium on the 29th of November.

One day I had to go back to Luneville, and was met at the front entrance by an MP. He asked if I could spare an hour in the Administration Building. This is an hour I'll never forget.

The room was packed with officers, and I was given the only seat left close to the interrogation table. A Major with master stripes was at a table with a table in front of the interrogation table; he'd spent years teaching English at the University of Hamburg, and knew every German dialect of the country.

As a prisoner was ushered into the room, he stood and saluted the soldier and then sat down. Then the soldier routinely raised his hands and said "My nomen is…" and gave his serial number and rank in his company. The Major gave him a cigarette and spoke to him nicely. He asked the prisoner where he lived and other routine questions, and then started in a more serious inquisition.

When a storm trooper came in a black outfit, he was usually very brusque to let you know that he was of the elite units. However, the Master Sgt, or Major, always asked the questions he wanted and received the answers he wanted.

In one case, a solider had just been brought from the front. He had a battered trench coat on, mud on his shoes, and bandanna tied around his head with some blood on it. The Major started with the usual cigarette, let the solider sit down, and after asking him several questions, became a little more brusque and finally, had him stand, and took the cigarette from him. The Major accused him of lying about where he was captured and where he was fighting. At this point, two officers stood and studied the map where the soldier claimed he was when he was captured. There was yelling about this, as the soldier swore he was telling the truth as he was pointing on the map. The Major gave him back his cigarette.

At this point, the two officers that stood to see where the soldier was pointing, they noticed that he had just pointed out an ammunition supply location that the Air Corps had been trying to locate for several days!

They said that the Major got the data he wanted from every soldier he interviewed. He would go from a whisper to a smile, to talking very briskly, and to shouting to the point that he would scare all the people in the room, especially the prisoner, in order to get the answers he sought.

It was a fitting conclusion to my stay in France, and one I will never forget.

ESNEUX, BELGIUM

We moved into Esneux just before Thanksgiving, coming through Bastogne. Although the weather was cool and cloudy, it wasn't long until the weather changed and the Belgian Bulge began. We could hear gunfire regularly, and we were prepared to move at any time, with little warning. Our challenge was to repair roads and any airfields in the area.

From Luxembourg to Aachen, the land in German was hilly and wooded. The Germans took all of the trucks and jeeps they had that were American, gathered all of the people who spoke perfect English, established them as troops and came into our area as American soldiers.

The first time we recognized what was going on was when one of our Sergeants asked one of their leading soldiers a question, as the soldier was answering he pointed outward, and his German Army uniform underwear peeked out from under his sleeve!

We were routinely bombed by buzz bombs. When one landed within one-quarter mile of our dynamite, we had to destroy the entire cache.

We were quartered in a mansion at the top of a hill, and we also had the river bridge mined for dynamiting.

On 24 December, Captain Wiedeman called us officers for a special meeting and said: "This is TOP SECRET. We are leaving for Germany TOMORROW." That is all he would tell us. That afternoon was the first day that the clouds cleared, as for the entire month of December the clouds covered the Belgian Bulge site, the temperature hovered around zero degrees, and it snowed… it was the most trying days for our troops and we lost many men during this time.

The afternoon of the 24th, with it clearing skies, we had many fighter planes in France and for the first time the bombers from England could fly to help the battle-weary soldiers of Bastogne. At one time I counted seven planes coming down at one time, as the German planes met our planes just overhead at Esneux. One of the planes was a B17 bomber, and the crew bailed out just as the plane exploded.

That night, a dance was scheduled. We decided to continue and host the dance, as cancelling it might raise suspicion. At one point, I danced with a girl I'd met previously. She said to me, "Vous partez pour Allemagne demain, oui?" (You're leaving for Germany tomorrow, aren't you?) I denied this and she told me exactly where we were going, staying and where the airfield was going to be built. It finally became the first airfield built by American troops in Germany. To this day, I don't know where she got the information, or if she was spying, pumping me for additional information.

We left for Germany on Christmas Day.

AACHEN

We arrived and set right to work in the cold, snow, and mud. When we were crossing the Rhine River, we had 62 P47s take off within 12 minutes. They flew two abreast of each end of the runway. The wind was mild so it didn't bother the planes, and it was great to see their return. The airfield was completed and was being used as a fighter base.

After crossing the railroad bridge at Remagen, we moved into Sinzig. Our duty was to unload supplies from trains, including food and other items for troops at the front. We also unloaded building materials, for plans being constructed on-site. One of the large prisoner-of-war bases was set up south of Remagen, also near Sinzig. I was left with my platoon to unload these cars, and send the material forward. In doing so, I became the Senior Officer and Military Governor in Sinzig, and so the problems of the community and my platoon were daily problems.

One day, the burgomeister's secretary came over and said, "We build furniture, and have many cords of drying lumber stacked nearby. The infantry are using it for firewood. Will you please contact them as we promise we will deliver all of the wood they need for fire, but save our valuable lumber." The comment of the infantry Captain when I made the request to him, wasn't fit to print, but he did acknowledge the problem and they began only using the firewood provided by the city.

On another day, a German civilian came to me and asked me to come downtown to settle a case, because they had a troublemaker in the store. I went with him. It was a men's store with handkerchiefs, ties, and shirts in the front, and suits and heavier clothing in the rear. The store had many older women standing in the front of the store, and the troublemaker was with the owner in the rear. The person was dressed in fatigues, looked to be in his older twenties, and the person who asked me to come settle the problem was the interpreter.

I was speaking in English and the troublemaker was speaking in Polish. I soon found out that what I was telling him in English was being relayed by the interpreter, but what the Polish man was saying in German was not being translated into English. So I said to the Polish man, "Sprechen Sie polnisch?" (Do you speak Polish?) To this he replied, "Po Polsku ja rozumie,"(Yes, I speak Polish) and then we conversed in Polish, and the German interpreter didn't understand.

He explained that he was a slave worker, had German marks (money), and wanted to buy something in the store. He said that while the Germans were in power, if the store owner sold a Polish slave worker something, he would be killed for doing so, but now that the war was over he wanted to buy something using the money he had earned as wages. I took some coins from the storeowner and put them in my hand, and then I took some of the coins of the Polish worker in my hand. I shook my hand and opened my hand to the storeowner and said, "Which coins are yours and which are from the Polish worker?" They were the same. I told the storeowner, "They are the same and anyone can purchase things at your store using these coins." I told the Polish man, "Sure, you can purchase something," and all of the people in the store, except for the interpreter who still did not understand us, cheered. From that day on people were able to purchase the food and supplies they needed without prejudice.

At that time in Germany, I could get by in Polish, French, German, Russian, and Czechoslovakian.

One day before I left, the Burgomeister came to the office with his secretary. He presented a parade sword that was his son's, a pilot in the Luftwaffe, who was killed over Berlin. He said, "I would like to give this to you, in appreciation for what you have done for my people."

All of history is full of the D-Day landing. We left Tulln Airfield in Vienna for our trip home. There were no festive parties, our unit was listed as staying to complete the airfield for national use, but after hearing that they were sending troops home with 75 points, then men in our company sent a cablegram to their Senator telling him that we were staying with 110 points, and they wondered why. The very next day, we were on our way home. It didn't take long to load our trucks for the trip to Le Havre.

With all the money spent in combat and D-Day publicity, our D-Day, or date of departure, was different. We went to France to leave our trucks at any Army depot and then boarded the freight cars that were featured in World War I for our trip home. There were no facilities of any kind on board, and every train stop for food was welcome. Traveling time consisted of sitting on the floor or your barracks bag, I don't know the distance but we were glad to get to Le Havre, and the ship we were going to be taking home. I was surprised at how much different the high tide was from the low tide.

It took several days for the entire group to arrive, so we spent the time talking or playing cards. It took us four days to cross the ocean to Boston, and a great relief to be on the way HOME… in October 1945.

When I arrived in Chicago, my dad picked me up for the joyful ride home. ✧

Michael J. Wohead (Mike Wohead), U.S. Army Aviation Engineers, Co A 818th Engr AVN BN, 1941 to 1945. Drafted 21 October 1941. Defended the west coast after Pearl Harbor, 7 December 1941. Promoted to First Lieutenant and served in the European Theater (England, France, Belgium, Luxembourg, Holland, Germany and Austria) building runways, providing air support and, when necessary, demolition of bridges for Patton's Army. Involved in major battles building runways prior to the battle commenced, often under Nazi and Allied Forces fire. Battle of the Bulge, D-Day +16, built the first US Airstrip in Germany, participated in capturing the Remagen Bridge to prevent the Nazi advance into France which enabled the Allies to start the final push toward V-E Day. Lead Battalion to free many European villages at conclusion of the war.

When the war ended, he was with his platoon south of Remagen, near Sinzig, Austria. He was the Senior Officer and became the Military Governor of Sinzg and surrounding areas. He worked with the German people as well as the Polish, French, Russian and Czechoslovakian, who were former prisoners or from work camps. On the day before he was leaving, the Burgomeister came to his office and gave him the parade sword of his son, a Luftwaffe Pilot, who was killed over Berlin. He stated, "I would like to give this to you in appreciation of what you have done for my people." Mike returned home in October 1945. ✦

Michael J. Wohead

26 W 165 Bauer Road

Naperville, IL 60563

In Memoriam

CPL Nick Roush; 1987 - 2009

THE GUARD

It was darkness. A gust blew down the rocky hills to the valley defining the area. Morning had only a hint in the eastern sky, as it climbed the far slopes. Dust was gently whipped up in the air and thrown yards away, over and over again. An empty road wound its way through the valley, and disappeared as it ran from blackness to blackness. Only the wind held its own against the silence.

Then came a sound.

As if from nowhere, several footfalls disrupted the gravel and a group made its way across the dry terrain. Seven men walked slowly along the road, making only the quietest noise with each step. Their pace was easy but deliberate. The man in front held up his hand and the company stopped. Walking several more steps the man glanced around and turned back to the others.

"Here," he said in a deep tone; his voice steady in contrast to the uneasy landscape. Without another word being spoken the rest of the men moved to form a circle around the first; three on one side of the road, and three on the other. Facing outwards they fixed their stares on the surrounding hills. In the center, the leader seemed to bow his head slightly, and for several minutes the men stood motionless, moving not so much as an arm to wipe the sand from their faces. As the dawn progressed, several stray rays found their way over the hills and cast a dim glow on the silent band of men. For a moment they could be seen; standing with faces fixed in an unearthly sternness, it was a company of soldiers.

Seven feet was the shortest height in the entire group, some were even taller. Each one had dirty blond hair with matching beards that clung close to their faces. Their eyes were different shades of blue, and set deeply behind their defined cheekbones. Their brows were bent into a firm gaze that affirmed a sturdy demeanor. They were all heavily muscled and broad-chested. Each one was in full battle dress. Each donned desert camouflage; their sleeves rolled up to their elbows. The leader wore a blue and white checkered pashmina closely around his neck. They were all packed with ammunition magazines, knives, side arms, grenades, and two were lashed around their torso with bandoleers of rifle rounds. Each bore an assault weapon slung on their shoulder, with an index finger resting on the stock an inch away from the trigger. They were locked, loaded, and ready for combat. Then the light was extinguished by black clouds that raced in from down the road, and the dark returned.

A deep hum could now be heard from somewhere in the dark. The men remained unmoved as the hum developed into an incessant rumble. Louder and louder it came. Raising his head, the man in the center glanced behind him for a moment, and then took his place on one side of the road. As he stepped off the beaten path, a Humvee ripped through the center of the group. A rumbling shook the very earth, but the men kept their footing. Stones and dirt were tossed everywhere. A cloud of dust enveloped the area. Moments later a second vehicle sped through, continuing the disruption of the earth. Then above the deafening roar of engines came a voice from the group.

"Ready!" it bellowed loud and clear above the noise.

A flash.

For a moment the area became bathed in white light. The noise eclipsed even the sound of the vehicles. An explosion shredded any silence left in the valley. An approaching Humvee was hit. Sound of flying metal whistled sharply as it was shot into the dark. The vehicle went on end; tossed upright, spun on two wheels, and fell to its side; finally coming to rest directly in the center of the group of soldiers. A fire broke out, illuminating the scene. A ghostly glow reflected off the disturbed dust. The seven soldiers were silhouetted around the destroyed Humvee.

"Contact!" one bellowed, and he leveled his weapon to the night. The black hills exploded in a cacophony of ungodly howls. Screams of anger and rage filled the valley from one end to the other. Black wisps of human forms descended on the small group of soldiers. They circled around and around the wreckage, moaning their hungry screams at the men. The soldiers dropped to one knee; with their cheeks pressed firmly against their rifle stocks they trained their weapons outward, and began engaging. All seven men began firing into the mass of figures.

Bullets tore into the dark enemy. Their forms contorted in ungodly fashions as they fell into nothingness.

"Reloading!" one shouted, and tossed his spent magazine to the ground. The others could be seen firing, quickly jerking to find new targets. Six-pointed muzzle flashes burned the dark again and again. The men who had emerged from the wreck paid no heed to the soldiers fighting only feet away. The black mob circled, unwilling to penetrate the perimeter the men had secured.

Suddenly a man stepped from the black horde. He was larger than the rest and stood at least ten feet tall. Clothed in black battle dress he walked casually towards the circle. The commander held up a fist and shouted the cease fire order. Keeping his rifle aimed at the dark figure's head, he allowed him to advance. As the scene quieted the two men could be heard conversing in their own language. The dark figure's gestures suggested he was pleading his case to the soldier. With a smile he pointed towards the burning vehicle and held up his palms in expectation of delivery. Having not moved his weapon the entire time, the soldier could faintly be heard giving his response;

"He is our man."

Fire filled the dark man's eyes and he produced a scream so loud that it seemed his vocal chords would shred themselves. In response the dark army howled in tune to its leader. Tremors shot through the ground as the world began to shake.

Then silence.

Unmoved through the entire ordeal, the leader of the soldiers shot a look around the scene before shouldering his rifle. The other men retained their positions on the perimeter. Moving to the Humvee, the leader stooped to the door and held his hand out in a beckoning gesture. From out of the wreck a hand grabbed the soldier's. With a yank the soldier hauled a man from the flames. He was unscathed. His look was not unlike the seven. He donned camouflage and a ball cap, but his hair was shorter, and his beard scantier – and they were both red. The blond soldier snapped to attention and saluted the other.

"My orders are to get you home," he explained. Together, the six other soldiers shouldered their weapons and saluted. The red-haired soldier looked at them and produced a knowing smile.

"Let's go," he said confidently. A gust blew past the men and nearly put out the flames. When the fire snapped back to its position, the valley was empty. And the wind held its own against the silence.

— Curt Batdorff

"He will command His angels
concerning you, to guard you…" Psalm 91:11

IN ORBE TERRUM NON VISI

Your courage and sacrifice will never be forgotten.
Rest In Peace.

Killed In Action
SGT Christopher P. Abeyta (USA), March 15, 2009 in Nangarhar
SSGT Timothy Bowles (USAF), March 15, 2009 in Nangarhar
SPC Norman Cain, III (USA), March 15, 2009 in Nangarhar
SGT David M. Caruso (USMC), November 09, 2004, Fallujah
PFC Ervin Dervishi (USA), January 24, 2004, Baiji
SPC James Powell (USA), October 12, 2003, Baiji
MAJ Douglas Zembiec (USMC), May 11, 2007, Baghdad
SPC Robert M. Weinger (USA), March 15, 2009, Nangarhar

Passed Due To Injures Related To Military Service
CPO Joey "Toolman" O'Toole (USN, Retired), May, 2010
MSGT Eden Pearl (USMC), December 20, 2015
SGT Lukasz Saczek (USA), May 10, 2009
The 27 military personnel who lost their lives on March 19th, 1982 in a KC-135
  accident near Greenwood, Illinois.

BROTHERS IN ARMS FOUNDATION

Brothers In Arms Foundation was founded in 2009 and is a volunteer and veteran-operated nonprofit organization. We provide financial and logistical support to disabled veterans, active duty, and immediate family members of Marines & FMF Navy Corpsman who have been wounded, fallen ill, Fallen or injured while serving within the Special Operations Community of The United States Marine Corps. Originally established to provide immediate support to four wounded MARSOC Marines and their families after they sustained near fatal injuries in Afghanistan in 2009, we now support multiple active duty Marines, Corpsman and veterans throughout the country.

Brothers In Arms provides assistance with travel, relocation, medical needs, childcare and funeral assistance not covered by military or related insurance. We also support the modification of homes to better facilitate the needs of disabled veterans and active duty servicemen. In addition to family specific programs, we also assist wounded Special Operations Marines and Corpsman in the following ways:

- Donate/purchase airfare, food/lodging and transportation to Service Members, Veterans and family members visiting wounded Marines in rehabilitation hospitals throughout the World.
- Provide travel assistance to family members of wounded, Fallen, ill or injured Service Members and Veterans.
- Purchase medical supplies for wounded Service Members and Veterans recovering at home.
- Donate money to special projects supporting Service Members and Veterans.
- Donate money to families needing assistance with relocation due to a family member in a rehabilitation hospital.
- Relocation assistance not covered by The U.S. Military.
- Childcare assistance during relocation.
- Home modifications assistance for Service Members and Veterans disabled in the line of duty.

Phillip Noblin, Founder and Volunteer Director

Phillip served eight years in Force Reconnaissance, and the Special Operations Community of the United States Marine Corps, and is a Combat Veteran of Operations Iraqi and Enduring Freedom. Additionally, Phillip served as a Direct Action, Special Reconnaissance Instructor at the Marine Special Operations School. Phillip continues to support his military community as the Founder & Executive Director of the Brothers In Arms Foundation. Phillip is co-founder and the Chief Financial Officer of Invictus Security, a South Florida based private security firm.

US VETERANS FOUNDATION

US Veterans Foundation is an organization focused on establishing a community presence through service-oriented programs that benefit the military community as well as general communities as a whole. USVF strives to ensure that our Veterans are mentally fit and equipped with all the tools required to make them very productive members of our communities and great community leaders. Our key objective is to combat the epidemic of Veteran suicide, statistically at 22+ per day, by providing a support network with enriching opportunities.

US Veterans Foundation was formally established in September of 2014, registered in Illinois as a Not For Profit Organization and classified by the IRS as a 501(c)(3) Public Charity. USVF campaigns to raise money to bring about change for the betterment of our Veteran community. We are headquartered in Alton, IL, founded and operated by Veterans, and dedicated to helping our returning military service members with their transition to the civilian world. The founding members of US Veterans Foundation are military Veterans of Iraq and Afghanistan wars, Desert Storm, and Vietnam era conflicts.

Oftentimes, our returning Veterans face challenges unfamiliar to the civilian world. Working through camaraderie assists with re-integration into the civilian world, identification of opportunities through networking, and opportunity for mentoring our younger Vets by those of us who have already been through the transition. Therapeutic programs give Veterans a sense of accomplishment and camaraderie, and viable alternatives to long-term medication. USVF provides support and solidarity to our Veteran community through outdoor adventures, service dog resources, and morale-enhancing events.

The organization is open to ALL US military Veterans, active duty, Guard and Reserve, and those who wish to support the military community.

There is a belief shared within the organization that every Veteran who has honorably served deserves the future opportunities, quality of life, and dignity that they themselves have fought to defend. We want to help Veterans realize these goals. We want to make a difference. We at the US Veterans Foundation have adopted the motto "One Team, One Fight." Our goal is to help Veterans truly come home and realize that we are one team, and one family. Help us reach that goal. Join us. Fight for their lives; help us make the difference.

Jason Thompson, Board Member and
Chief Executive Officer